THE WINTER'S TALE

NOTES

including
- *Life of the Author*
- *Source and Background*
- *Brief Synopsis*
- *List of Characters*
- *Summaries and Commentaries*
- *Review Questions*
- *Selected Bibliography*

D1007813

by
Evelyn McLellan, Ph.D.
University of Nebraska

WILEY

Wiley Publishing, Inc.

About the Author
Gary Carey, M.A.
University of Colorado

Consulting Editor
James Roberts, Ph.D.
Department of English
University of Nebraska

Publisher's Acknowledgments

Production
Wiley Indianapolis Composition Services

CliffsNotes™ *The Winter's Tale*
Published by:
Wiley Publishing, Inc.
909 Third Avenue
New York, NY 10022
www.wiley.com

CONTENTS

THE WINTER'S TALE NOTES

LIFE OF THE AUTHOR

Many books have assembled facts, reasonable suppositions, traditions, and speculations concerning the life and career of William Shakespeare. Taken as a whole, these materials give a rather comprehensive picture of England's foremost dramatic poet. Tradition and sober supposition are not necessarily false because they lack proved bases for their existence. It is important, however, that persons interested in Shakespeare should distinguish between *facts* and *beliefs* about his life.

From one point of view, modern scholars are fortunate to know as much as they do about a man of middle-class origin who left a small country town and embarked on a professional career in sixteenth-century London. From another point of view, they know surprisingly little about the writer who has continued to influence the English language and its drama and poetry for more than three hundred years. Sparse and scattered as these facts of his life are, they are sufficient to prove that a man from Stratford by the name of William Shakespeare wrote the major portion of the thirty-seven plays which scholars ascribe to him. The concise review which follows will concern itself with some of these records.

No one knows the exact date of William Shakespeare's birth. His baptism occurred on Wednesday, April 26, 1564. His father was John Shakespeare, tanner, glover, dealer in grain, and town official of Stratford; his mother, Mary, was the daughter of Robert Arden, a prosperous gentleman-farmer. The Shakespeares lived on Henley Street.

Under a bond dated November 28, 1582, William Shakespeare and Anne Hathaway entered into a marriage contract. The baptism of their eldest child, Susanna, took place in Stratford in May, 1583. One year and nine months later their twins, Hamnet and Judith, were christened in the same church. The parents named them for the poet's friends, Hamnet and Judith Sadler.

Early in 1596, William Shakespeare, in his father's name, applied to the College of Heralds for a coat of arms. Although positive proof is lacking, there is reason to believe that the Heralds granted this request, for in 1599 Shakespeare again made application for the right to quarter his coat of arms with that of his mother. Entitled to her father's coat of arms, Mary had lost this privilege when she married John Shakespeare before he held the official status of gentleman.

In May of 1597, Shakespeare purchased New Place, the outstanding residential property in Stratford at that time. Since John Shakespeare had suffered financial reverses prior to this date, William must have achieved success for himself.

Court records show that in 1601-02, William Shakespeare began rooming in the household of Christopher Mountjoy in London. Subsequent disputes over the wedding settlement and agreement between Mountjoy and his son-in-law, Stephen Belott, led to a series of legal actions, and in 1612 the court scribe recorded Shakespeare's deposition of testimony relating to the case.

In July, 1605, William Shakespeare paid four hundred and forty pounds for the lease of a large portion of the tithes on certain real estate in and near Stratford. This was an arrangement whereby Shakespeare purchased half the annual tithes, or taxes, on certain agricultural products from parcels of land in and near Stratford. In addition to receiving approximately ten percent income on his investment, he almost doubled his capital. This was possibly the most important and successful investment of his lifetime, and it paid a steady income for many years.

Shakespeare is next mentioned when John Combe, a resident of Stratford, died on July 12, 1614. To his friend, Combe bequeathed the sum of five pounds. These records and similar ones are important, not because of their economic significance but because they prove the existence of William Shakespeare in Stratford and in London during this period.

On March 25, 1616, William Shakespeare revised his last will and testament. He died on April 23 of the same year. His body lies within the chancel and before the altar of the Stratford church. A rather wry inscription is carved upon his tombstone:

Good Friend, for Jesus' sake, forbear
To dig the dust enclosed here;
Blest be the man that spares these stones
And curst be he who moves my bones.

The last direct descendant of William Shakespeare was his grand-daughter, Elizabeth Hall, who died in 1670.

These are the most outstanding facts about Shakespeare the man, as apart from those about the dramatist and poet. Such pieces of information, scattered from 1564 through 1616, declare the existence of such a person, not as a writer or actor, but as a private citizen. It is illogical to think that anyone would or could have fabricated these details for the purpose of deceiving later generations.

In similar fashion, the evidence establishing William Shakespeare as the foremost playwright of his day is positive and persuasive. Robert Greene's *Groatsworth of Wit,* in which he attacked Shakespeare, a mere actor, for presuming to write plays in competition with Greene and his fellow playwrights, was entered in the *Stationers' Register* on September 20, 1592. In 1594 Shakespeare acted before Queen Elizabeth, and in 1594-95 his name appeared as one of the shareholders of the Lord Chamberlain's Company. Francis Meres in his *Palladis Tamia* (1598) called Shakespeare "mellifluous and hony-tongued" and compared his comedies and tragedies with those of Plautus and Seneca in excellence.

Shakespeare's continued association with Burbage's company is equally definite. His name appears as one of the owners of the Globe in 1599. On May 19, 1603, he and his fellow actors received a patent from James I designating them as the King's Men and making them Grooms of the Chamber. Late in 1608 or early in 1609, Shakespeare and his colleagues purchased the Blackfriars Theatre and began using it as their winter location when weather made production at the Globe inconvenient.

Other specific allusions to Shakespeare, to his acting and his writing, occur in numerous places. Put together, they form irrefutable testimony that William Shakespeare of Stratford and London was the leader among Elizabethan playwrights.

One of the most impressive of all proofs of Shakespeare's authorship of his plays is the First Folio of 1623, with the dedicatory verse which appeared in it. John Heminge and Henry Condell, members of Shakespeare's own company, stated that they collected and issued the plays as a memorial to their fellow actor. Many contemporary poets contributed eulogies to Shakespeare; one of the best-known of these poems is by Ben Jonson, a fellow actor and, later, a friendly rival. Jonson also criticized Shakespeare's dramatic work in *Timber: or, Discoveries* (1641).

Certainly there are many things about Shakespeare's genius and career which the most diligent scholars do not know and cannot explain, but the facts which do exist are sufficient to establish Shakespeare's identity as a man and his authorship of the thirty-seven plays which reputable critics acknowledge to be his.

SOURCE AND BACKGROUND

No one seriously disputes Shakespeare's source for *The Winter's Tale.* Convincing internal evidence links his play to *Pandosto: The Triumph of Time,* a popular novel by Robert Greene, first published in 1588.

Shakespeare follows most of Greene's narrative for the first three acts of *The Winter's Tale,* but he changes the names of all the characters whom he adapted from Greene. Two favorite characters, Autolycus and the shepherd's son, are Shakespeare's creations, as are his radical changes in Acts IV and V. In such rural settings as the sheep-shearing scene in Act IV, Shakespeare adds to Greene's less developed pastoral theme, and in Act V, Shakespeare restructures Greene's ending to achieve a more satisfactory romantic conclusion. According to most critics, Shakespeare's play was probably written during the years 1610-11. One certain date is a performance recorded on May 15, 1611.

As a play written at this late stage of Shakespeare's career, *The Winter's Tale* can be given two important classifications: it is more Jacobean than Elizabethan, and it is more Romance than Comedy, History, or Tragedy.

The Jacobean classification is actually a subclassification of the entire span of years which is commonly referred to as the Renaissance. The Jacobean period extends from 1603 (the year of Elizabeth's death) to 1642 (the year when the Puritans closed the theaters); the term is taken from the name of King James I, who ruled from 1603-25 (*Jacobus* is the Latin form of the name James). Two key characteristics of the age are the widening (1) political and (2) religious splits between the Cavaliers and the Puritans, a conflict which degenerated into Cromwell's takeover and led to dominant attitudes of realism and cynicism.

Perhaps this influence of realism and cynicism partially accounts for Shakespeare's altered vision in his final four plays. These plays, so difficult for critics to classify, are often referred to as the "problem plays." They are sometimes interpreted as a third step in Shakespeare's tragic cycle – an addition of the concept of renewal to the themes of prosperity and destruction which Shakespeare explored in his tragedies. According to this interpretation, in *The Winter's Tale* Shakespeare reveals King Leontes' destruction of his happiness when Leontes confuses his jealous imagination with reality; then the playwright finally reconstructs the family and the happiness of Leontes, after Leontes has passed a sufficient number of years in sincere repentance.

The four plays in this group of "problem plays" are *Pericles, Cymbeline, The Winter's Tale,* and *The Tempest.* Two centuries ago, these plays were variously classified as either a history, a comedy, or a tragedy. The ambiguous label "tragi-comedy" might also apply to this group because some of their shared characteristics are: happy endings, which might be described as revelations; elements of the supernatural, combined with Christian resurrection; themes of sin, expiation, and redemption; and father-daughter pairings in which the daughter precipitates reconstruction after the breakdown of family unity.

In *The Winter's Tale,* the daughter, Perdita, certainly symbolizes *spring* and *renewal* throughout the play, and her mother, Hermione, is "resurrected" from a living death as a statue. Furthermore, this play shares with the other three a portrayal of love that transcends the unrealistic, total merriness of the comedies to a more realistic somberness that incorporates both natural mutability and the occasional sadnesses which love imposes.

Another genre which is identifiable in these plays is that of the pastoral romance, but they should not be confused with escapist literature; they contain serious lessons about virtue and vice. Yet they are not hampered by strict insistence upon verisimilitude. The plots are deliberately far-fetched, and the stories feature both the astounding and the incredible. Thus, Shakespeare's creation of "a seacoast" for Bohemia can be excused as perfectly suitable to the genre.

Other conventions of the Romance help explain events in *The Winter's Tale* which might otherwise strike the twentieth-century reader as being false or ridiculous. These conventions include mistaken identities, supernatural events, and ideal poetic justice and courtly settings, even among the lower classes. One might note also that the characters often act without concern for motivation; indeed, critics have raised serious questions about the apparent absence of motivation in these plays, especially after Shakespeare had developed psychological masterpieces in the tragedies that were written earlier. For that reason, it is important to determine whether or not the characters *earn* their happy endings or if the playwright merely *grants* them.

An important idea in these plays which has not changed from Shakespeare's earlier plays was the notion of the Order of the Universe, which he structured in accordance with popular Elizabethan beliefs. One image used to represent this view of Order is the great Chain of Being. In this Chain, each link represents some single thing in Creation. All things were linked, beginning with the foot of God's throne and ending with the humblest inanimate object. Together, they all formed a unity of the Universe with an order determined by God. The top three links represented God, the Angels, and Mankind. But as high as they are on the Chain, the Angels and Mankind were not supposed to regulate or alter the Order. Instead, the Order of the Heavens was supposed to be duplicated on Earth.

With this in mind, consider the impossibility of altering the ultimate role of Perdita (Leontes' lost daughter) in the Order which was determined by God. She is meant to live as royalty, even after she is raised by a rustic shepherd. Not surprisingly, she is credited by everyone with possessing the qualities of a queen. And in spite of his great powers, Leontes is not able, finally, to alter her destiny — that is, to live and eventually to reign.

Leontes' power to exercise Free Will is an important part of the concept of the Order of the Universe. The belief that God granted the power of Free Will to Angels and to Man helps to explain the exceptions to the remarkable Order. Free Will was believed to be available, and it could be used incorrectly — to the detriment of the individual's responsibility to contribute to the orderly maintenance of the Universe. Leontes is a good example of this improper use of Free Will.

Another exception to this ordered structure was Fate, conceived of as being uncertain and subject to disorders in the Universe. The phenomena of these disorders was often represented by the Wheel of Fortune, horoscopes, and the stars. The turning wheel and the moving stars were believed to influence man's existence, with man frequently a helpless participant. Again, Free Will offered the means to challenge Fate, if anyone was willing to risk punishment by exercising it to challenge the operation of the Universe.

A key corollary to this orderly view of the Universe was the phenomenon often described as the Cosmic Dance. This Neoplatonist concept embraced the Greek representation of creation as being like music; it viewed the operations of the universe as being akin to a perpetual dance to mystical music; the planets, the stars, and other living things were all dancing on individual paths and different levels, but coalescing finally in cosmic harmony. (The different levels corresponded to the Great Chain of Being.) Of particular interest for *The Winter's Tale* are images of dancing seas and Perdita's "dance of nature."

Another image that is also significant is the dance of the body politic, suggested by the movement of the courtiers around Leontes and, later, the festival participants around Perdita.

BRIEF SYNOPSIS

Archidamus, a lord of Bohemia, and Camillo, a lord of Sicilia, talk about their respective countries. Archidamus says that if Camillo were to visit Bohemia he would discover great differences between their countries. Camillo replies that he thinks that his king, Leontes, is planning a trip to Bohemia in the summer. Abashed by how little Bohemia has to offer in comparison to Sicilia, Archidamus imagines himself serving drinks that would make the visitors so sleepy that they would not notice the barrenness of Bohemia. The lords also discuss the lifelong friendship of their two kings, as well as the virtues of the two young princes.

Camillo then joins a group which is composed of the two kings, Leontes and Polixenes, Leontes' family, and some attendants. Polixenes, King of Bohemia, is thanking Leontes for his extended hospitality in Sicilia and insisting that he, Polixenes, must return to his country's responsibilities. When it is clear that Polixenes will not yield to Leontes' entreaties to stay for a longer visit, Leontes urges his wife, Hermione, to join the effort. Hermione succeeds in persuading Polixenes to stay.

Leontes seems delighted that Hermione has convinced Polixenes to stay, but suddenly he reveals that he is jealous of Polixenes. Seeing that Leontes is upset, Hermione and Polixenes ask him what is wrong. Leontes, however, avoids a truthful answer by claiming that he is merely remembering when he was the age of his son. The two kings then compare their love for their sons.

Leontes takes a walk with his son, Mamillius, thinking that this will set up Polixenes and Hermione for a compromising situation. Hermione, however, innocently discloses where she and Polixenes will be, and Leontes indulges in satiric swipes at her imagined infidelity. Then he sends Mamillius off to play, before asking for Camillo's assessment of the relationship between Hermione and Polixenes. Camillo's straightforward responses, however, are twisted by the jealous king, and Camillo protests: the imagined bawdiness which Leontes interprets from his wife's and Polixenes' actions is *wrong*. The king lashes out at Camillo, and Camillo humbly begs for a reappraisal of his reliability as an observer for the king. When Leontes insists upon a confirmation of Hermione's infidelity, a shocked Camillo criticizes his king.

Leontes then tries to extract an agreement that his list of observed actions (between Hermione and Polixenes) *proves* that his wife's and Polixenes' affair is a reality. Camillo urges the king to heal "this diseased opinion," but Leontes *cannot* be convinced. He suggests that Camillo poison Polixenes. Camillo admits that he *could* do it, but he states that he will never believe that Hermione was unfaithful. Camillo agrees to poison Polixenes *if* Leontes promises not to reveal what he believes about Hermione. Leontes promises, then joins the innocent couple.

Alone, Camillo speaks of his hopeless position. Approached by Polixenes to explain Leontes' changed attitude, Camillo convinces Polixenes that they must flee together or they will both be killed by Leontes.

Act II opens some time later with an obviously pregnant Hermione resting in the company of her son, Mamillius, and two ladies-in-waiting. When Hermione requests a story, Mamillius suggests a tale about "sprites and goblins," a tale suitable for winter.

As Mamillius begins the story, Leontes and Antigonus enter with a group of attendants. Leontes clearly believes that the hasty departure of Camillo and Polixenes is confirmation of his suspicions about Hermione's affair with Polixenes. He orders Mamillius to be kept away from his mother, and he accuses Hermione of being pregnant by Polixenes. Ignoring Hermione's protests, Leontes orders her to be imprisoned. She bravely accepts her fate and exits with the guards.

Beset by protests from his astonished advisers, Leontes insists that they refuse to see the evidence before them. The king quiets the protesters by revealing that he has sent for an interpretation from the oracle at Delphos.

After the birth of Hermione's baby (a girl), Paulina, the wife of one of the lords of Sicilia, Antigonus, attempts to persuade Leontes to retract his accusations as she presents his beautiful, innocent baby to him. But she selects a poor time to approach Leontes. He has just stated that *killing Hermione* would allow him to sleep again, and he has resolved not to worry about his sick son lest he be distracted from his commitment to revenge. Paulina refuses to listen to the warnings of her husband and her attendants. Instead, she stubbornly tries to convince Leontes that the baby is *his.*

Leontes, however, responds as Paulina was warned he would. Her arguments in favor of the queen and baby escalate his tyranny. He then tries to pit Antigonus against Paulina, ordering him to take the bastard child and Paulina away. Antigonus protests that no man can control his wife. When Leontes orders that the baby be thrown into a fire, Antigonus negotiates a chance for the baby to live – if Leontes will spare the baby's life, Antigonus promises to do *anything* that Leontes requests. Vowing to kill both Paulina and Antigonus if Antigonus fails to obey, Leontes orders Antigonus to take the baby to a remote place and abandon her to Fate. Antigonus doubts that this "fate" is better than a quick death, but he agrees to leave the baby to the mercy of wild animals, and he exits to carry out Leontes' command.

No sooner has Antigonus left than a servant announces the return of the messengers from Delphos.

Act III opens with Cleomentes and Dion talking about the awesome experience which they shared at Delphos. Both men hope that Apollo has declared Hermione innocent, and they hurry off to deliver the sealed message from the oracle.

Leontes orders that his wife be brought in to hear the reading of the oracle's decision, fully expecting that she will be found guilty as charged and, thus, he will be cleared from the stigma of tyranny. Cleomentes and Dion swear that they have brought the message from Delphos without breaking the seal.

The message declares that Hermione, Polixenes, Camillo and the baby are *all* innocent. It further states that Leontes is "a jealous tyrant" and asserts that "the King shall live without an heir, if that which is lost be not found." Leontes declares that the message contains no truth, and he orders the trial to proceed. Just then, a servant announces that Mamillius has died. Hermione seems to faint, and Paulina announces that the news has killed the queen.

Leontes repents and orders Hermione to be tended to with the belief that she will recover. He then announces his intention to make peace with his old friend Polixenes, to woo Hermione, and to recall Camillo. He declares Camillo a good and faithful servant who was right to disobey his order to poison Polixenes.

Paulina enters, wailing over the death of Hermione and attacking Leontes for his dreadful, tyrannical edicts. She says that the king should embark on a life of repentance as a result of what he has done to his family. Leontes replies that he deserves all that she has said and more. Paulina then expresses regret for her attack because she detects the remorse which the king is feeling. She says she will remind him no more of the death of Hermione and his two children.

Leontes asks that he be taken to view the bodies of his dead wife and son. He declares that they shall share the same tomb, and he vows that he will visit the tomb each day to weep.

In the next scene, we discover that Antigonus and the infant are still alive, for Antigonus is seeking assurance that his ship has indeed arrived at "the deserts of Bohemia." He and a seaman look at the sky and agree that a brewing storm may portend heavenly anger if they abandon the helpless infant; they also agree that they do not like their task. Antigonus promises to hurry.

Antigonus then describes his nightmare to the infant. Her mother, he says, appeared to him in a dream, a figure of sorrow. The dream figure requested that he leave the baby in Bohemia and that he name her Perdita. Then she informed him that because of this task, he would never again see his wife. Antigonus concludes that Hermione is dead and that Polixenes *is* the father of the baby. After uttering best wishes for the baby and regret for his actions, Antigonus runs off stage, chased by a bear.

A shepherd enters, despairing the wenching and fighting of all male youths between the ages of ten and twenty-three. When he sees Perdita, he assumes that she is an abandoned child born out of wedlock. He pities the baby so much, though, that he decides to keep her. The shepherd then calls for his son, who is identified in the script only as "clown." The boy tells his father about two sights that have shaken him—the drowning of an entire crew of a ship (the one that brought Antigonus and Perdita to Bohemia) and a man (Antigonus) consumed by a bear. The shepherd turns his son's attention to the baby, whom he surmises is, somehow, linked to a fortune. The boy opens the baby's wrappings and discovers gold. Urging his father to take the baby home, the boy is inspired by their sudden good fortune to return and bury the remains of Antigonus.

The Chorus narrates that a bridge in time occurs at the opening of Act IV, and it also summarizes the highlights of an interim of sixteen years. Then, Polixenes and Camillo enter in the middle of an argument about Camillo's decision to return to Leontes after his long sixteen-year separation. Polixenes warns him that returning *could* be fatal to Camillo. Besides, *he* needs Camillo. Camillo, however, wants to return to his native country for he is growing old, and he thinks that he can comfort the now-repentant Leontes.

Polixenes agrees that his penitent "brother" has a sad history, but asks consideration for his *own* sad lot—that is, having a son who is "ungracious." Camillo acknowledges that he has not seen the prince (Florizel) for three days and does not know where the young man spends his time. The king says that he has been informed that Florizel spends a good deal of time at the home of a shepherd who has somehow acquired great wealth. They both guess that Florizel must be attracted to the shepherd's beautiful young daughter. Polixenes persuades Camillo to help him discover what Florizel is up to.

Autolycus then enters, singing a song of hope and high spirits. He identifies himself as a peddler of oddities, and also as one who makes his living by cheating fools. On cue, the "clown" (the shepherd's son) enters, trying to calculate his budget and remember his shopping list for the upcoming sheep-shearing feast.

Autolycus dupes the clown by pretending that he has been beaten, robbed, and then clothed in his despicable rags. The clown is sorry for Autolycus and offers him money. Then he hastens off to buy his supplies. Autolycus chortles about lifting the clown's purse and exits.

The scene which follows focuses on the sheep-shearing feast. Florizel and Perdita flounder in an awkward courtship. Florizel praises Perdita's qualifications as the chosen "queen" of this spring ritual. But aware of Florizel's being a true prince, and the unreality of her title as "queen," Perdita is unhappy. She cautions Florizel about the potential wrath that a liaison between them might arouse in his father. Florizel urges her to remember some of the mythical transformations that love has caused.

As Perdita again urges the prince to be realistic, he swears to honor his love for her above all other things. He then commands her to exhibit cheer for her approaching "guests."

Perdita's "father," the shepherd, chides her for neglecting her duties as a "queen." Therefore, Perdita begins entertaining; first, she greets the disguised Polixenes and Camillo and hands out flowers to them. After the king and his adviser observe Perdita's prudent parries to Florizel's bold courtship, Polixenes observes a bearing and beauty in Perdita which transcend her supposedly low station. Camillo affirms these unusual qualities. The clown moves the festival into action by calling for music and dance, and again, Polixenes remarks upon Perdita's grace. The shepherd says that the young couple love each other and hints that "Doricles" (Florizel's pseudonym) will discover an unsuspected dowry if he proposes to Perdita.

The entertainment continues with a dance of twelve satyrs performed by a group of uninvited amateurs, but throughout these dances, Polixenes observes Florizel and Perdita. Deciding that it is time to part the couple, the king calls Florizel over to ask why he did not bring presents to enliven his romance. The love-struck prince declares that Perdita does not care for such trifles; she wants only gifts which are locked in his heart.

When Florizel declares that no power or wealth could seem worthwhile without Perdita's love, Polixenes and Camillo support the sentiment. The shepherd then asks his daughter if she feels the same way. She says that she does but cannot express it as well.

The shepherd declares the betrothal of the young couple, with the two strangers as witnesses. The disguised Polixenes urges Florizel to consult his father before making such an important decision, but Florizel impetuously and repeatedly refuses. Enraged, Polixenes casts off his disguise and threatens to punish all who participated in the betrothal without consulting him.

Perdita sighs that she was afraid something like this would happen. She urges Florizel to make up with his father and never return to her. The shepherd, in great confusion and despair, berates the young people for the ruin and the wretched death which they have probably condemned him to. But Florizel stubbornly clings to Perdita and tells his father to go ahead and disinherit him.

When Florizel decides to take Perdita and flee in a ship anchored nearby, Camillo stops him, advising him to make peace with his father. Then Camillo begins laying a plot to try and eventually return to Sicilia himself.

Camillo convinces Florizel to marry Perdita so he can present himself with his new bride to Leontes in Sicilia. He predicts that Leontes will welcome the opportunity to be the host for the son of the long-separated "brother," since Polixenes will not respond to Leontes' invitation to end their old quarrel. Florizel agrees that this plan seems preferable to wandering forever as unwelcome strangers in strange lands. Camillo then offers funds from his wealth in Sicilia to properly outfit the royal party.

Act V is set again in Sicilia. Leontes is seemingly much the same man as he was when we last saw him sixteen years before. He is conversing with Paulina and the two lords who brought the message from Delphos, Cleomenes and Dion. Cleomenes is urging Leontes to forget and forgive his evil "as the heavens have done." But Leontes says that as long as he can remember those whom he lost, especially Hermione, he cannot forget his errors.

Paulina, we see, is still feeding Leontes' guilt. Cleomenes and Dion ask Paulina to "stop salting the wounds." She retorts that their wish for the king to heal so that he can marry again counters Apollo's oracle "that King Leontes shall not have an heir/ Till his lost child be found," an event as unlikely as the return of her own husband, Antigonus. She tells Leontes not to wish for an heir.

Leontes *encourages* Paulina to continue to remind him of Hermione's superior virtues; he believes that taking any other wife would end in disaster. Paulina extracts an oath from Leontes, in the presence of the two witnesses, that he will *not* marry until Paulina approves. Paulina states that such a time will come *only* when Hermione is re-created.

A servant enters then to announce the arrival of Prince Florizel and his wife, whom he describes as a woman unsurpassed in beauty and virtue. Leontes cleverly perceives that Florizel's small group of attendants means that this visit is "forced." It is not an official visit, at all. Paulina notes the servant's excessive praise of Florizel's wife. She chides him for such praise when he has written verses that have stated that Hermione could *never* be equalled. The servant, however, maintains that all will agree with him after they have seen Perdita.

Leontes is thrown into a miserable reminiscence when he sees the young couple. They remind him of his loss of friendship with Polixenes. Florizel claims that his father sent him to reinstate that old friendship; Polixenes, he says, is too infirm to make the trip himself, and he then relates an imaginary tale about his strange arrival. He says that he has arrived from Libya, where he acquired Perdita. He explains the small group that accompanies him by saying that he sent the larger group to Bohemia to report his success to his father. He then requests that Leontes remember his own youthful love as good reason to petition Polixenes' acceptance of Perdita. Leontes, reminded of his love for Hermione, promises to speak for the young couple.

In the next scene, Autolycus questions some gentlemen who possess important news from the court of Leontes. The stories are pieced together to reveal that Leontes now knows that Perdita is his daughter and that he can finally celebrate the return of his lost heir.

Because of Perdita's request to see the lifelike statue of her mother, a celebration dinner has been organized near the statue.

The final scene at Hermione's statue is the setting for the play's "renewal." When they first enter, Leontes is suffering, but Perdita steadfastly stares at the lifelike statue. Paulina then amazes them all by commanding the statue to move. At last, Hermione speaks, and everyone learns that she has remained alive (but hidden) all these sixteen years. As they all exit to enjoy their new happiness, Leontes ends Paulina's loneliness by choosing the good Camillo to be her husband.

LIST OF CHARACTERS

Leontes

The King of Sicilia. As noted by Polixenes at the beginning of the play, Leontes has everything that love, loyalty, family and power can provide – until he is dominated by jealousy and tyranny. After he has caused those most dear to him to die and disappear, he repents for sixteen years until he is ready to be offered a second chance for happiness. When he is again given the opportunity for love and loyalty, he is ready to cultivate and encourage these qualities, because he now understands and appreciates their values.

Mamillius

Young son of Leontes; Prince of Sicilia. At a young age, Mamillius is wrenched away from his mother and forbidden to see her again. The moody, precocious boy dies, presumably of a broken heart, before his mother's sexual fidelity and innocence is accepted by his father. Mamillius' death seems, to Leontes, to be a punishment by the gods and causes Leontes to realize that his persecution of his wife has been a horrible mistake.

Camillo

A lord of Sicilia with a natural inclination to be a valuable friend. After he decides to join Polixenes rather than kill him, Camillo becomes just as valuable an adviser to the Bohemian king as he had been to Leontes. He is also wise and skilled enough to reconcile the love between Polixenes and his son, Florizel, into a tapestry of reunion and reconciliation among all the surviving, original sufferers in the play.

Antigonus

Another lord of Sicilia. He seems to be the most influential lord in Leontes' court after Camillo leaves. Unfortunately, he does not possess the necessary skills to counter the chaos and madness caused by Leontes' temporary tyranny. He cannot control his wife, Paulina, nor can he contrive a humane fate for the infant Perdita. He deserves sympathy, however, for trying his best and for placing Perdita in the right place at the right time for both survival and a return to the life for which she was born. Antigonus suffers more than circumstances justify, however, when he is chased and devoured by a bear.

Cleomenes and Dion

Two more lords of Sicilia. Their most important role in the play is to fetch and deliver the oracle's message from Delphos.

Polixenes

King of Bohemia and childhood friend of Leontes. When Leontes ends their friendship, Polixenes develops in a different and more wholesome way. But he has his own personal crisis, which involves the perfidy of his son, Florizel. Unlike Leontes, Polixenes seeks advice at the time that he seeks facts, and although Polixenes ignores advice at the climax of his crisis, his wise choice of an adviser and his absence of tyranny eventually contribute to the concluding reconciliation at the end of the play.

Florizel

The son of Polixenes; Prince of Bohemia. A brash and high-spirited young man, he is willing to throw away all responsibilities, loyalty, and filial love in exchange for the chance to live with and love Perdita. Because he listens to Camillo and cares about Perdita, he is able to emerge from his ardent, youthful fantasy without destroying anyone. But he is tempted by headstrong emotions, a key to his character — that is, he is capable of being selfish and self-centered.

Archidamus

A lord of Bohemia who plays no further role after he has described the barrenness of Bohemia in the opening scene.

Old Shepherd

The shepherd who finds and raises Perdita. For some reason, he has no name. Although he does appropriate the gold that was left with his foundling "daughter," he otherwise seems to raise Perdita in a fair and nurturing atmosphere. For instance, no character is aware of any different treatment or attitude toward his "real" child and his "foster" child.

Clown

The son of the old shepherd also exists without a name. Identified only as the traditional clown role that he fills in the play, the character is developed enough to be a remarkable favorite for generations of audiences.

Autolycus

Another favorite character from this play. A rogue who had once served Prince Florizel, he lives and delights by his wits. He plays a minor but key role in the final reconciliation; and when the good-hearted clown promises to reward Autolycus, the groundwork is prepared for our feeling that rewarding the rogue is more just than punishing him for his earlier thievery.

A Mariner

He exists long enough to transport Perdita to Bohemia, regret his actions, and die in a storm.

Hermione

Queen of Sicilia; the wife of Leontes. Russian by birth, this character is an unbelievably pure combination of virtues, including a sufficiently patient optimism which sustains her through sixteen years while she hides and waits for the right moment to rejoin her repentant husband. She never utters a sigh or a word of remonstrance about the loss of her children or her freedom after she forgives Leontes.

Perdita

The daughter of Leontes and Hermione; Princess of Sicilia; later, the wife of Florizel, and Princess of Bohemia. Without any environmental influence, she grows up with a quality of royalty being one of her most innate traits and with an uncanny resemblance to her mother in behavior as well as appearance. Her outstanding virtue is common sense, which Florizel needs from their union more than he ever seems to realize. This quality is also used effectively to bring authenticity to a character who would otherwise be only two-dimensional.

Paulina

Wife, then widow of Antigonus. A loyal lady-in-waiting to Hermione, she voices the conscience of Leontes in an irritating and scolding tone. But she is unarguably diligent and, therefore, she deserves her final reward of marriage to the good Camillo.

Emilia

Another attendant of Hermione.

Mopsa and Dorcas

Two shepherdesses who dramatize the role models for young women of their social level; they fail to sway Perdita from her natural inclinations toward graciousness and gentility.

Chorus

The Chorus makes a mid-plot appearance in order to provide an exposition of the interim of sixteen years.

SUMMARIES AND COMMENTARIES

ACT I – SCENE 1

Summary

Archidamus, a lord of Bohemia, tells Camillo, a lord of Sicilia, that should he ever visit Bohemia that he would find great differences between the two countries. Camillo responds that he thinks his king plans an exchange visit during the coming summer.

Archidamus predicts that although their entertainments cannot match Sicilia's, they will manage to express their love. When Camillo protests the apology, Archidamus emphasizes that he knows that his country of Bohemia cannot produce "such magnificence." Archidamus then envisions offering drinks that will drug the visitors; if unable to praise their hosts, they will at least not be able to blame them for inadequate "magnificence."

Camillo then tells Archidamus that Leontes (King of Sicilia) is being so generous because of the great love that he has had for the Bohemian king since childhood. All of the formal, diplomatic gifts which the kings have exchanged during the intervening years of separation have maintained the strong friendship that still binds them. Camillo calls for help from the heavens to maintain this love.

Archidamus comments that no earthly force could be strong

enough to alter that love. Then he praises Leontes' son, Prince Mamillius, as the most promising young man he has ever observed. Camillo agrees, claiming that Leontes' elderly subjects remain alive only for the joy of observing Mamillius when he grows to adulthood. Archidamus, more realistically, states that the elderly would find a reason to continue to survive even if Mamillius did not exist.

Commentary

The conversation between Archidamus and Camillo establishes the two main settings of the play (Sicilia and Bohemia) and introduces the theme of deep and lasting friendship between the two kings. We can also infer that Leontes possesses natural riches far beyond those of Polixenes (the king of Bohemia). The fact that no single main character appears in this scene forces our initial focus onto the contrasting settings; Sicilia is established as being the preferable location.

While Archidamus bemoans the impossibility of matching the hospitality of Sicilia, he introduces a human temptation which will cause great harm throughout the play—that is, confusing reality with illusion. First, he is stymied by reality: "We cannot with such magnificence—in so rare—I know not what to say." Then, he envisions a means to avoid the reality: "We will give you sleepy drinks, that your senses, unintelligent of our insufficience, may, though they cannot praise us, as little accuse us." A little later, Archidamus reverses his vision and returns to reality, when he counters Camillo's claim about Mamillius: "They that went on crutches ere he was born desire yet their life to see him a man." Archidamus doubts that the elderly would die without the inspiration of Mamillius, and he bluntly declares: "If the King had no son, they would desire to live on crutches till he had one."

Archidamus then speaks of the long friendship between the two kings, and he says that he doubts if there is "in the world either malice or matter to alter it." In fact, no *reality* does exist to alter that friendship, but *illusion* can, and will, alter it.

ACT I—SCENE 2

Summary

Leontes, his wife Hermione, Polixenes, Camillo, and a bevy of lords stroll quietly on stage. Polixenes announces that after nine months away from his royal duties, he must return home tomorrow. Leontes urges Polixenes to stay at least another week, but Polixenes insists that he must leave the following day to tend to his duties, although no one could touch him so emotionally as Leontes can.

Leontes then urges his wife to speak. Hermione reassures Polixenes that all is surely well in Bohemia; otherwise, he would have heard by now. Thus, he is free to stay. When Polixenes continues to resist the invitation to stay, Hermione declares that he *will* stay, either as her guest or as her prisoner. Given that choice, Polixenes agrees to stay one more week.

Polixenes then enters into a reverie of his boyhood with Leontes. Hermione is curious about Leontes at that age. Polixenes recalls that they were both innocent, as alike as lambs. When teased about their loss of innocence, Polixenes graciously explains that neither of them had yet met the women whom they would eventually wed. Hermione then asks if their wives made them sinners or if they had sinned with others.

Noticing the liveliness of their conversation, Leontes calls out: "Is he won yet?" Hermione responds that Polixenes *will* stay. Leontes congratulates his wife on her power of speaking convincingly, saying that only once before has she spoken so well. Hermione is intrigued and asks when was the other time. Leontes responds that it occurred at the end of their courtship when she said, "I am yours forever." Hermione responds that the first time she spoke well earned her a husband; the second time, a good friend.

Hermione extends her hand to Polixenes, and they walk away from the others. Leontes fumes over every small gesture which the couple makes. He interprets impropriety, and he calls his son over and unleashes a mixture of double entendres with dirty innuendos. Enraged by jealousy, Leontes examines his son for signs of illegitimacy. Recognizing his emotional distress, he proclaims "the infection of my brains/ And hardening of my brows."

Concerned about the change in Leontes' appearance, Polixenes and Hermione ask him if he is all right. Leontes lies, saying that while he was looking at Mamillius, he was reminded of his own "lost" youth. Leontes then asks Polixenes if he is fond of *his* son. Polixenes describes both the frustration and the pride of fatherhood, but despite them both, he says that his son means everything to him.

Leontes claims that his son means the same to him. He states that he will walk with his son awhile and urges Polixenes and Hermione to walk elsewhere. Hermione says they will walk to the garden where they can be found if Leontes wants them. After watching the couple's actions, Leontes lashes out at his son: "Go play, boy, play. Thy mother plays," adding that she will "hiss" him to his grave. Clearly, the Sicilian king is convinced that his wife is unfaithful – as are most wives – in *his* estimation.

Noticing Camillo, Leontes asks him for his version of what has happened. Camillo answers that Polixenes would not stay when Leontes asked him to do so, but changed his mind when Hermione entreated him. Leontes thus assumes that Camillo and others are already whispering about his cuckoldry. But when pressed to confirm Hermione's infidelity, Camillo is shocked, and he criticizes his king. After Leontes attacks Camillo's character and his reliability as a witness for not admitting or noticing that Hermione is "slippery" and a "hobby-horse," Camillo retorts: "You never spoke what did become you less than this."

Unable to force Camillo to agree with him, Leontes slips into the role of a tyrant. He orders Camillo to poison Polixenes. Camillo agrees this would be easy enough, especially since he is Polixenes' cupbearer, and he promises to poison Polixenes *if* Leontes promises to treat Hermione as though nothing has happened – for the sake of their son and for the purpose of forestalling international gossip. After Leontes agrees, Camillo urges Leontes to join Polixenes and Hermione and to seem to be friendly with them. Camillo then reveals to us that he is all too aware what happens to men who would poison a king.

Polixenes enters confused and asks Camillo for an explanation of Leontes' unfriendly behavior; Camillo refers vaguely to a sickness. Polixenes presses Camillo for a clearer explanation, and Camillo finally admits that he has been ordered to poison Polixenes because the king suspects him of philandering with Hermione.

At first, Polixenes wants to confront Leontes, face-to-face, with a denial, but he is persuaded by Camillo that this would be as useless as forbidding "the sea . . . to obey the moon." Finally, Polixenes accepts Camillo's plan for them to secretly slip away in small groups, and he promises Camillo asylum in return. As Polixenes remembers the rarity and purity of Hermione, he fears that Leontes' insane jealousy of Polixenes will result in violence. The two men then exit to begin their hasty escape.

Commentary

As hinted by Archidamus in the previous scene, nothing which is real in *this* world is altering the present situation. Incoherence now even afflicts Leontes:

> Then 'tis very credent
> Thou may'st co-join with something; and thou dost,
> And that beyond commission, and I find it,
> And that to the infection of my brains
> And hardening of my brows.
>
> (I.ii.142-46)

Leontes' jealousy in this scene is the key to the quality of the conflict, the probability, and the development of both plot and character throughout the play. The onset of Leontes' jealousy comes without warning, motivation, or justification. Leontes' first jealous reaction is: "At my request he would not," meaning that Polixenes was not swayed by Leontes' entreaties. This statement is reinforced when Leontes reminds Hermione that she had spoken to equally good purpose when she promised him, "I am yours forever." Significantly, since Hermione and Polixenes are both innocent, they both fail to detect the rivalry and the jealousy which Leontes is now displaying.

To Leontes, everything which the couple does inflames him; he assumes that they are flaunting their attraction for one another.

Most damaging of all to Leontes is his increasing self-seduction by illusion. Observing some innocent courtly handplay, he spits out: "Too hot, too hot!/ To mingle friendship far is mingling blood."

Suspecting even the illegitimacy of his son, Mamillius, Leontes imagines the snickering whispers of everyone about his cuckoldry "Inch-thick, knee-deep, o'er head and ears a forked one!" He tells Mamillius, sarcastically, to go "play," like his mother, and then he indulges in his fantasies, telling himself that many men consort with their wives without realizing that "she has been sluiced in 's absence." He concludes that the problem must be widespread because there is no medicine, no protection against it:

> No barricado for a belly: know 't;
> It will let in and out the enemy
> With bag and baggage.
>
> (I.ii.204-06)

At this stage, the innocent charm of his son and the reality offered by Camillo can no longer link Leontes with reality. Thus, the Sicilian king sinks further and further into illusion:

> Is whispering nothing?
> Is leaning cheek to cheek? Is meeting noses?
> Kissing with inside lip? stopping the career
> Of laughter with a sigh? – a note infallible
> Of breaking honesty; – horsing foot on foot?
> Skulking in corners? wishing clocks more swift?
>
> (I.ii.284-89)

In vain, Camillo pleads for Leontes to quickly "be cured of this diseased opinion" because of its danger.

Here, Leontes turns to tyranny, a transformation which is extremely dangerous because of the power which he commands during his sickness. He commands Camillo to verify the truth of his observations. Camillo refuses. Leontes insists, "It is; you lie, you lie!/ I say thou liest, Camillo, and I hate thee." Stoking his power with anger, he orders Camillo to poison Polixenes. It is no wonder that Camillo perceives himself in a hopeless dilemma and thus turns to Polixenes for help. When Polixenes correctly interprets Camillo's allusion to "a sickness/ Which puts some of us in distemper" (jealousy because of suspected adultery), the Bohemian king clearly understands the hopelessness of the situation:

> This jealousy
> Is for a precious creature. As she's rare,
> Must it be great; and as his person's mighty,
> Must it be violent.
>
> (I.ii.451-54)

Affirming the queen's innocence, Polixenes can only wish her well and flee for his life.

The major conflict of the play begins to shape the plot: Leontes has flung himself against reality. He is willing to destroy his richest possessions – the love and loyalty of his family, his best friend, and his court advisers – for *revenge*.

We can understand Leontes' tyranny because of our knowledge that human nature, when inflamed by jealousy, is often a cause of murder. In addition, Leontes' extraordinary power increases his capacity to murder. Camillo and Polixenes are sufficiently developed as characters to realize that their interpretations of reality leave them helpless before the sick illusion of the king's jealousy. The protests which the audience might feel because their observations of reality conflict with Leontes' conclusions are contained in the protests of Camillo.

Shakespeare's stage and acting directions are superb aids for actors during these scenes. For instance, the friendship between the two kings is keenly illustrated with action: "They have seemed to be together, though absent; shook hands, as over a vast; and embraced, as it were, from the ends of opposed winds." Note, too, Shakespeare's clues for the actions of Hermione and Polixenes are ones which must sufficiently motivate Leontes. Entertwined with the warm sharing of childhood memories, these two must act out an enticing, inciting scene of "paddling palms," "pinching fingers," and laughter cut short. This dramatization increases in significance with the knowledge that Shakespeare altered the truly imprudent behavior of Hermione in his source and substituted, instead, the simple, innocent action of hand-play to incite Leontes' jealousy.

Although no truly exciting action occurs in this scene, the dramatic pace quickens with the infusion of the king's perverted emotions. Jealousy, and then fear, shatter the peaceful, sleepy grace of the first scene.

One other central idea is subtly introduced in this scene. With the seemingly minor theme of youth, Shakespeare begins building the key theme of *rebirth* – one of those concepts which separates this group of final plays from the tragedies.

As a brief review, remember that Camillo believes that the elderly subjects of Sicilia stay alive merely to experience the promise of Mamillius' youth; remember also the strength of the bonds formed during the innocent youth of the two kings. More specific to the purpose of resolving Leontes' disease, notice references to the healing power of youth, such as "physics the subject" and "makes old hearts fresh." Later, when Perdita emerges as the symbol of spring and rebirth, she will belong to a tradition within the world of the play.

ACT II – SCENE 1

Summary

Although Hermione and Mamillius enter together, Hermione immediately turns to her ladies-in-waiting and asks them to take the boy. Mamillius immediately engages the ladies with his precocious wit.

One lady teases Mamillius about how much he will want their company after the new prince is born. The second lady observes that Hermione appears to be filling out rapidly, and she wishes her a speedy delivery.

Hermione asks what they are talking about, then she asks her son to tell her a tale. "Merry or sad?" asks her son. "As merry as you will," Hermione responds. Mamillius decides, "A sad tale's best for winter." Hermione encourages him to try to frighten her with his sprites since he is good at that. Teasingly, he whispers the story to her so that the ladies-in-waiting cannot hear it.

Leontes enters with Antigonus and some other lords, just as Leontes is receiving news of the departure of Camillo and Polixenes. He interprets their sudden departure as verification for his accusations, and he says that he finds the knowledge as odious as seeing a spider in a cup from which he has just drunk.

Since Camillo was with the departing party, Leontes states that there must indeed be a plot against his life and his crown. In addition, he declares that Camillo must have been employed by Polixenes *prior* to the plan for poisoning; now, he fears what plots their combined knowledge will inspire them to hatch. Puzzled about how they got through the gates, he is informed that Camillo used his keys.

Leontes demands that Hermione give Mamillius to him. Saying that he is glad she did not nurse him, he declares that already she has too much of her blood in him. Astonished, Hermione asks if this is some kind of game. As an answer, Leontes orders Mamillius to be taken out and kept from his mother; cruelly, he adds that Hermione can amuse herself with the child by Polixenes, the one whom she now carries.

Hermione denies that the unborn child is Polixenes' and states that she believes her word should be enough to dissuade Leontes from his jealous accusations. Leontes announces to everyone that they may look at her and find her "goodly," but that they cannot find her "honest"; Hermione, he says, is an adulteress. Hermione reacts cautiously. Had a villain said that, she says, he would have become more of a villain, but Leontes is simply mistaken. In response, Leontes escalates his accusation. Not only is Hermione an adulteress, but she is a *traitor* – in consort with Camillo and Polixenes – and had knowledge of their plan to escape. Gently, Hermione denies the accusations and predicts that Leontes will grieve over his statements when he finally knows the truth. She says that he can make this up to her – but only by declaring his mistake. Leontes, however, is convinced that he has built truth from facts; he orders her to prison and says that anyone who speaks in her behalf will be judged to be as guilty as she is.

Hermione observes that "some ill planet reigns" and decides to be patient until the disorder is corrected. She tells the lords that, although she is not as prone to tears as most females are, she feels an "honorable grief." She asks the lords to judge her feelings but to obey their king. She then requests that her ladies accompany her to prison in order to help her with her pregnancy. Admonishing her ladies not to weep since there is no cause, she advises them to save their tears in the event that she should ever deserve to be sent to prison. As part of her graceful obedience, she tells Leontes that she never wished to see him sorry, but now she realizes that she will see him eventually very sorry.

The king orders them out, and Hermione leaves in the company of her ladies and guards. Immediately, the lords begin to argue against the king's order. Antigonus prophesies that Hermione, Leontes, and Mamillius will all suffer for this act. One lord wagers his life that the queen is innocent. Antigonus pledges to keep his wife in the stables if Hermione is proven guilty, because such a sin would mean that *no* woman could be faithful. Leontes tells them to keep quiet.

Antigonus says that he is sure that Leontes has listened to a liar, and he says that in addition to his pledge to keep his wife in the stables, he vows to geld his daughters to prevent any issue – if Hermione is proven guilty. Leontes again tells them to be quiet. He says that their senses are dead; only *he* feels and sees the issues clearly. All honesty, Antigonus says, is dead. Leontes is amazed that his lords do not trust his judgment. At this, one of the lords says that he would *prefer* to disbelieve his king than to accept this judgment; furthermore, he would prefer to believe in Hermione's honor than in Leontes' suspicions.

Leontes declares an end to all advice; since his lords do not seem to be able to discern truth, he will have to rely on his own "natural goodness" as judge and counsel. Calling upon royal prerogative, he reminds them that he need not seek their advice in the matter because he has all the power needed to proceed. Then he informs them that he has taken a step to curb any possible rashness; he has sent Cleomenes and Dion to Apollo's temple in Delphos, and he *promises* to abide by the spiritual counsel of the oracle.

When told that he has done well, Leontes quickly adds that he is convinced that he has acted correctly and really needs no more information; he trusts that the oracle will reassure those who cannot now perceive the truth. Meanwhile, Hermione will remain in prison so that she cannot carry out any treasonous plots left undone by the two who fled. Leontes calls on them all to accompany him as he publicly announces the events.

Commentary

This act's structure is similar to that of Act I. It opens with a sleepy, peaceful pace – which Leontes will soon shatter. Hermione requests a tale from her son, and Mamillius suggests a sad tale as "best for winter." A "winter's tale" means a story to pass the long evening hours of winter, especially a story that its listeners will enjoy when it is retold.

With Leontes' entrance and simultaneous reaction to the report about the escape of Camillo and Polixenes, the season of royal discontent disintegrates quickly into *general* discontent. Because of the play's title and because of Mamillius' "tale suitable for winter," the situation becomes reminiscent of Richard III's phrase, "the winter of our discontent." In effect, Leontes creates a perpetual winter's death without the hope of spring's rebirth and regeneration. Leontes eliminates the hope of rebirth and rehealing when he rejects his unborn child and when he isolates his son. In these "problem plays," rejection usually leaves only tragedy as the possible consequence of the destructive tyranny which Leontes has initiated. His disease must now progress untreated unless the circumstances change.

As Leontes destroyed his friendship with Polixenes in the previous act, he now destroys his family. Again, note that nothing that exists in their world justifies altering those relationships: *illusion* motivates Leontes. He alters everything to suit his sense of "justice," justice which he metes out unfairly because of misconstrued events.

With his jealous imagination still gnawing at him, Leontes leaps to an even more serious accusation against Hermione – treason. The facts from which he draws this conclusion, however, do not influence others to deduce the same conclusion. A lord reports that he saw Camillo, Polixenes, and Polixenes' attendants rushing to their ships. Immediately, Leontes exclaims: "How blest am I/ In my just censure, in my true opinion!" But Leontes fails to remember his own wicked, recently conceived poison plot! Pausing only to regret the knowledge he now has, he declares, with no further information:

> Camillo was his help in this, his pander.
> There is a plot against my life, my crown.
> All's true that is mistrusted. That false villain
> Whom I employed was pre-employed by him.
>
> (II.i.46-49)

As Polixenes predicted, Leontes' jealousy "for a precious creature" is enormous, and because of his powerful position, that jealousy now turns "violent." In fact, Leontes becomes increasingly paranoid. The disruption of his senses (his "nature") seems alarmingly probable. Declaring that sometimes it's better not to know unpleasant facts, Leontes illustrates this "truth" with fevered imagery similar to an unbalanced Lear:

> There may be in the cup
> A spider steeped, and one may drink, depart,
> And yet partake no venom, for his knowledge
> Is not infected; but if one present
> The abhorred ingredient to his eye, make known
> How he hath drunk, he cracks his gorge, his sides,
> With violent hefts. I have drunk, and seen the spider.
>
> (II.i.39-45)

This chilling image provides a clue to Leontes' insane-like disturbances.

Later, Leontes decides that Hermione is also involved in the non-existent plot against him.

> I have said
> She's an adultress, I have said with whom;
> More, she's a traitor, and Camillo is
> A fedary [confederate] with her . . .
>
> (II.i.87-90)

To Leontes, the causal sequences of Camillo's departure with Polixenes – immediately after Leontes' accusation that Polixenes committed adultery with Hermione – are proof enough that all three of them are involved in a treasonous plot. Of course, Leontes can provide no reasonable motivation for such a plot, and the audience is well aware that they have seen nothing to substantiate the accusation. Again, probability is maintained because the audience's evidence is firmly, unanimously supported by the arguing lords of Sicilia.

Leontes now escalates the tyranny that he first exhibited when he conspired with Camillo. As in the scene with Camillo, Leontes is suspicious of anyone who will not substantiate his illusions: thus, he unknowingly denies himself the benefit of more accurate, more truthful observations. Leontes refuses to listen to any opposing opinions. He even exhibits a streak of meanness when he pinches Antigonus; then he reveals even more of his evil nature when he forbids anyone to offer an opposing opinion as he sends Hermione to prison. After it becomes clear that the lords will not cease arguing, he calmly declares:

> Why, what need we
> Commune with you of this, but rather follow
> Our forceful instigation? Our prerogative
> Calls not your counsels, but our natural goodness
> Imparts this; which if you, or stupefied
> Or seeming so in skill, cannot or will not
> Relish a truth like us, inform yourselves
> We need no more of your advice.
>
> (II.i.161-68)

With this speech, Leontes now isolates himself with his insanity.

Confused because no one will accept his "evidence" or authority, his speech disintegrates into short, violent outbursts, sometimes barely coherent.

With everyone and every fact arguing against his actions, Leontes is clearly abusing and misusing Free Will. Hermione, in fact, concludes that "some ill planet" reigns; thus, she resigns herself to being patient until the heavens look with a more favorable aspect upon her.

All of this is the dramatic basis for the major conflict. We have witnessed the jealous, tyrannical Leontes as he flung his distorted illusions against reality. We watched Leontes escalate the willful destruction of his richest possessions. As a protagonist, he has severed his ties with his family and has isolated them; then he escalated his own isolation from the loyal advice of all who could have helped him see the truth. He has isolated himself from all *objective* communication, and finally he is left with only his own wrong illusions.

Suitably, the setting increasingly becomes a series of confined, isolated fragments. Hermione moves to prison, Mamillius is confined to his quarters, and Leontes places himself apart from anyone who disagrees with him. Characterization is of secondary interest in this scene. Leontes is developed almost as a stereotype to "Human Nature disrupted by Insanity." On the other hand, Hermione's goodness comes close to being unbelievable, were it not for the fact that we see her growing stronger, more self-sufficient, and patient—as do many pregnant women confronted with emergencies. Perhaps her unshakable pureness and goodness are essential in order to motivate all the underlings to argue with their king, but the audience may well wonder whether such a rare creature could actually exist beyond the stage of this play.

The age of Mamillius remains a mystery. Shakespeare portrays him as a spirited, flirtatious, proud and secretive youth—perhaps a young teenager. But his ties to his mother seem to indicate a much younger child. He lives, and soon dies, and he remains largely an inscrutable mystery.

ACT II—SCENE 2

Summary

Paulina and her attendants appear at the prison to request a visit with Hermione. The gaoler replies that he has orders not to allow visitors. Paulina then requests a chance to speak to one of the queen's ladies, Emilia if possible. The gaoler agrees to bring Emilia to Paulina if she dismisses her attendants, and if he himself can attend the conference. Paulina cooperates, but she expresses in asides the building fury which she feels about her good queen's imprisonment.

Emilia reports that Hermione is doing as well as one "so great and so forlorn" might expect in her situation. Blaming the fears and sadnesses that weigh upon the queen, Emilia reports the premature delivery of a daughter.

In spite of the "dangerous unsafe lunes i' the king," Paulina decides to show Leontes his infant daughter, and she pledges a blistering advocacy for the queen. If Hermione will trust her with the infant, Paulina feels that the sight of the innocent baby will persuade Leontes to change his attitude toward the queen.

Emilia praises Paulina as the most suitable woman to undertake the brave errand. In fact, she says, Hermione had thought of the same plan but had rejected it because she feared that anyone whom she might ask to do so would turn her down.

When Emilia exits to ask for the baby, the gaoler tells Paulina that he cannot allow the baby to leave the prison unless he sees a warrant. Paulina convinces him that the baby entered the prison as an innocent in her mother's womb and therefore needs no warrant in order to leave. This argument easily sways the simple gaoler, but Paulina further soothes his fears by pledging to stand between him and any danger from Leontes.

Commentary

Compared to Hermione's gentle, obedient reaction to Leontes' tyranny, Paulina's rage is graphically gathering as she prepares to confront her king. Obviously she has no intention of using the diplomatic ploys of Camillo or the other advisers; she will voice only her own absolute *outrage* at the mistreatment of the innocent. Well aware of the "lunes" (lunatic fits) which now control Leontes, Paulina determines that a direct attack of Truth will shake him loose from his insanity. And clearly, Leontes' actions can be called insane for they have destroyed a peaceful court life and a happy family life. The scene is focused on Hermione's hard and unjust imprisonment and Paulina's resulting rebellion: "Here's ado,/ To lock up honesty and honor from/ The access of gentle visitors." Paulina must claw her way into a position to argue the queen's case. She is not only a singular volunteer, but she is the most qualified person to do so, according to Emilia: "There is no lady living/ So meet for this great errand."

Paulina believes that she knows what Leontes really wants, and what truly motivates him. She believes that he *wants* to love his wife and child, but needs a new cause to do so. She is correct, but only after many tragedies and many years will this be proven. At present, Paulina chooses her own dangerous, unswerving course.

ACT II – SCENE 3

Summary

Leontes enters with a group of lords and servants – captives, really, who must listen to his ravings. He complains, first, that his inability to punish the traitors is causing him to suffer from insomnia. The "harlot king" – Polixenes – is out of reach, but at least Hermione is under control; now, if he could permanently free himself of her threat, he says, he believes that he might at least *rest* a little. He considers burning his wife.

When a servant reports that Mamillius may be finally recovering from his illness, Leontes says that the boy's problem is guilt about his mother's dishonor. The king then sends the servant to check on the prince and begins to rage about the power and the distance which make it impossible to revenge himself upon Polixenes and Camillo. He imagines at this moment that they are probably laughing at him.

At this moment, however, Paulina enters with the baby. When warned that the king has not slept and should not be approached, Paulina argues for the queen and for the *truth* that shall set the king free.

Leontes suddenly explodes at Antigonus for not controlling his wife. Paulina retorts that Antigonus can control her *dis*honesty, but not her *honesty*. Paulina pronounces herself a physician and a "counsellor." She champions Leontes' "good queen" and presents him with his baby.

Leontes reacts with a tantrum. He orders Paulina and "the bastard" removed. No one obeys, and so Leontes denounces all in the room as "traitors." Antigonus and Paulina both object to the charge. Paulina retorts that Leontes is cursed by his own slanders. Again, Leontes ridicules Antigonus as being henpecked. He then orders the baby and Hermione to be thrown into a fire. Paulina calls upon all present to mark the baby's resemblance to Leontes. In a frenzy, the king calls for Antigonus to be hanged because he cannot control his wife's speech. Antigonus replies that nearly all the husbands in the kingdom would have to die – if that is the punishment for a man who cannot control his wife.

Leontes then threatens to burn Paulina. She retorts: "I care not;/ It is an heretic that makes the fire,/ Not she which burns in 't." Careful to state that she is not accusing Leontes of being a *tyrant*, Paulina berates him for his "cruel usage of your queen,/ Not able to produce more accusation/ Than your own weak-hinged fancy"; she says that he is "ignoble" and "scandalous to the world." Leontes orders Paulina to be taken out of the chamber, then he defends his reputation by claiming that if he were a tyrant he would have killed her.

As she is pushed from the chamber, Paulina gives the baby to Leontes and tells everyone that humoring Leontes only makes his madness worse. Freed from Paulina's attacks at last, Leontes penalizes Antigonus for not controlling his wife by ordering him to burn the baby within the hour, or Antigonus and all his family will die. Should Antigonus refuse, Leontes promises to "dash out" the brains of the baby. Antigonus and all the lords swear that Antigonus did *not* send Paulina to attack Leontes. The king, however, declares them all liars.

The lords kneel and beg Leontes to repay their past loyal service by refusing to carry through his terrible plan. At first, Leontes contends that it will be better to burn the baby than to later resent her. But he gives Antigonus a chance to offer something in exchange for the baby's life. Antigonus offers anything "that my ability may undergo/ And nobleness impose." He even offers what "little blood" he has "to save the innocent."

Leontes presents a sword on which Antigonus is to swear that he will do *anything* ordered. Antigonus does so. Telling Antigonus to listen carefully because failure at any point will forfeit his own life and Paulina's, Leontes orders the old man to carry "the female bastard" to a remote place far from Sicilia where the baby must be abandoned. This action will leave the baby's life to Fate and circumstance. (Ironically, it will also offer the baby a chance for survival.)

Antigonus promises to do the king's bidding although instant death might be more merciful, he says. As he picks the baby up, he calls for "some powerful spirit" to instruct wild birds and beasts to nurse her and to bless this tiny innocent who is used so cruelly. As soon as Antigonus exits with the baby, Leontes mutters, "No, I'll not rear/ Another's issue."

A messenger announces the return of Cleomenes and Dion from the oracle at Delphos. All are amazed at the brevity of the twenty-three-day round trip. Leontes takes this as a sign that the oracle's message will support the truth that only he has deduced. He confidently orders the lords to prepare a "just and open trial" for Hermione during which the "truth" of his public accusations will be verified.

Commentary

Conflict never abates in this scene. Tensions build as everyone on stage contributes to the many attempts to resolve the complications. Leontes, however, continues to speak for *illusion,* while all the others speak for *reality.*

Leontes, the only character blinded by illusion, wants to throw Hermione, Paulina, and the baby into a cleansing fire. Already desperate from lack of sleep and absence of resolution, he cannot tolerate what is thrust at him by Paulina. In desperation, he orders her hauled from the chambers. That leaves only the baby to punish. He cruelly orders that the baby must be abandoned in a desolate spot where Fate may decide whether or not she lives or dies. These compromises on the lives of Paulina and the baby weaken the illusion that Leontes craves, so he looks forward to the proof that he believes will be contained in the oracle's message.

Paulina characterizes herself as a physician and counselor, one who has come to heal the torments caused by Leontes' illusions. She urges the king's advisers to realize that their *tolerance* of his moods only exacerbates the problem. Leontes, of course, finds Paulina intolerable. She increases his frenzy, and she cures nothing. However, she does prove that her brave confrontations with truth at least can curb the king's tyranny, for he cannot exercise his cruel orders until Paulina is removed from the scene.

Unfortunately for the king's family and his subjects, none of the lords follow her example. They continue to appeal to a reasoning power which no longer operates within him. In a final attempt to resolve Leontes' mad conflict, they kneel and beg for him to reward their past faithful service by sparing the life of the baby. Antigonus desperately promises to do *anything* to spare the baby's life. Their begging, however, inspires only more tyranny.

All the focus on the baby, however, does cause Leontes to change his order about her fate, but he does not really alter his cruel tyranny, and he manages to punish Antigonus for supporting his brave and loyal wife, as well as conceiving a cruel death for the innocent baby.

At this point, Leontes seems hopelessly desperate. He is insanely irrational; he wants revenge because he needs control. Instead of gaining control, however, every step he takes increases his own frenzy and diminishes all chances for help. Only by accepting reality, including his own contributions to the events, can Leontes regain emotional control of himself and his court.

Although the honesty of Camillo, Hermione, and Paulina prevent total mad tyranny, Leontes' frenzy increases. Leontes' "nature" can no longer tolerate any limits. He trusts no judgment but his own; thus, he blurts out: "You're liars all." The Elizabethan notion of the Order of the Universe which Leontes should be absolutely duty-bound to imitate has disintegrated before his mad illusions.

Only the oracle's message offers hope for resolution of the conflict.

ACT III – SCENE 1

Summary

Walking through the streets of a Sicilian town, Cleomenes and Dion exchange their impressions of the general appearance and, especially, the religious atmosphere that they observed on the "island of Delphos [Delphi]." Cleomenes remembers vividly the thundering voice of the oracle; Dion says that he hopes that the trip will prove as successful for the queen as it has for them. Both messengers are certain that Apollo's divination will clear up all doubts surrounding the accusations against Hermione. The two messengers exit to mount fresh horses in order to speed their delivery of the sealed message.

Commentary

At first glance, this brief scene seems to serve only as extraneous travelogue. It serves this purpose, but more important, it adds to the dramatic tension as preparations are being made for Hermione's trial. By verifying the "religious" authenticity of their visit to Delphos and by anticipating the divine perception of Hermione's innocence, the messengers seem now to bear an unimpeachable testimony against Leontes' tyranny.

As was mentioned earlier, the scene also employs the license which is recognizable in the Pastoral Romance genre when Delphos is described as an island.

ACT III – SCENE 2

Summary

Leontes expresses his grief to the lords and officers who enter the scene of the trial. Describing the accused Hermione as the daughter of a king, his wife, and also as someone who is "too much beloved," he urges the beginning of an open trial which can both clear him of all charges of tyranny and can determine Hermione's guilt or innocence.

After an officer opens the trial by announcing Hermione's personal appearance, the queen enters with Paulina and her faithful ladies-in-waiting. On Leontes' command, the officer reads the indictment. Hermione is formally "accused and arraigned of high treason" for committing adultery with Polixenes, conspiring with Camillo to kill Leontes, and then both advising and aiding "them, for their better safety, to fly away by night."

Hermione responds that, so accused, she can do little but deny the accusations. She realizes that a plea of "not guilty" will serve little purpose since her integrity has already been "counted falsehood." Instead, she builds this hypothesis into her argument:

>   If powers divine
> Behold our human actions, as they do,
> I doubt not then but innocence shall make
> False accusation blush, and tyranny
> Tremble at patience.
>
>   (III.ii.29-33)

She calls upon Leontes to remember, as the one who best can, her

years of true and faithful behavior. Hermione cites her credentials —
the daughter of a great king, and the mother of a "hopeful prince" —
and in contrast to the humiliation of pleading publicly for her life and
honor, she says that as much as she values life and honor, she will-
ingly *risks both* by requesting specific proof from Leontes in this public
forum, to cite even *one* incident from her life before — or during —
Polixenes' visit, which justifies the charges.

Leontes mutters about the general impudence of criminals. True,
agrees Hermione, but she cannot agree that the generality applies to
her. You just won't admit it, answers Leontes. Hermione says that
she admits only the *facts*. First, she loved Polixenes in a way suitable
to their rank and honor, as Leontes had commanded her to do. Refusal
to do so would have been classified as "disobedience and ingratitude"
toward both him and his childhood friend. Second, she has no experience in treason. She knows only that Camillo was an honest man.
If the gods know no more about his departure than she does, even
they must be able to guess why.

Again, Leontes responds with generalities. Hermione despairs of
understanding him. "My life stands in the level of your dreams,/ Which
I'll lay down."

Leontes rants, "Your actions are my dreams." Again, he voices his
jealousy, disguised as a legal charge: Hermione has a bastard daughter
by Polixenes; thus, she is past shame or truth. As surely as the infant
was cast out, shamed because no father would claim it, so shall Hermione suffer the pangs of justice. The easiest of her punishments will
be death.

Hermione requests respite from Leontes' taunts. The death threat
with which he tries to frighten her is the very thing she now wants.
Life holds no comfort now that her most worthwhile achievement,
his favor, is clearly lost, although the reason for the loss is not clear.
Also lost is her second joy, the company of their son, and her third
joy, the innocent baby daughter who was murdered before she was
weaned.

Hermione then lists other experiences that now make death at-
tractive to her. She has suffered from public accusations about her
immorality and from the cruel denial of care during childbirth, for
which women of all classes yearn. Finally, before she has recovered
from childbirth, she has been rushed to this open-air public trial.
Accordingly, what lure of life should cause her to fear death?

However, as willing as Hermione is for Leontes to proceed with the death sentence, she still yearns for the honorable memory that she deserves:

> If I shall be condemned
> Upon surmises, all proofs sleeping else
> But what your jealousies awake, I tell you
> 'Tis rigour and not law.
>
> (III.ii.112-15)

In a ringing challenge to all who judge her, she exhorts: "Apollo be my judge!"

One of the lords agrees that her request is just, so he calls for the oracle's message.

During the bustle of officers leaving the trial to fetch Cleomenes and Dion, Hermione expresses how much she yearns for the presence of her dead father, the Emperor of Russia, so that someone would regard her with "pity, not revenge."

An officer then swears in Cleomenes and Dion, who attest to the condition of the untampered, sealed message from Delphos. Leontes orders the breaking of the seal and the reading of the message. An officer reads: "Hermione is chaste; Polixenes blameless; Camillo a true subject; Leontes a jealous tyrant; his innocent babe truly begotten; and the King shall live without an heir, if that which is lost be not found." The lords and Hermione praise Apollo.

Leontes asks: "Hast thou read truth?" The officer confirms it. Then, Leontes declares, "There is no truth at all i' th' oracle./ The sessions shall proceed; this is mere falsehood."

A servant bursts in to announce, reluctantly, that Mamillius has just died from anxious conjecture about his mother's fate. Leontes cries out: "Apollo's angry; and the heavens themselves/ Do strike at my injustice."

Hermione faints. Paulina examines her, then commands Leontes to watch as Hermione dies. Leontes orders that Hermione receive tender care until she recovers. Remorsefully, he confesses that he has "too much believed mine own suspicion." After a party carries Hermione out, Leontes beseeches Apollo to forgive his profanity of the oracle. In a burst of clarity, Leontes promises to earn again the love of Hermione and to restore Camillo to office. Recognizing the damage done by his jealous quest for revenge as well as the probability that Camillo fled because of Leontes' command to poison Polixenes, Leontes praises the glowing honor of Camillo: "How he glisters/ Through my dark rust!"

Immediately after Leontes' confession, Paulina enters, consumed with hysterical grief. She confronts the "tyrant": the consequences of Leontes' jealousy should cause *him* to flee in despair. Paulina then catalogs the harm caused: betraying Polixenes, dishonoring Camillo for refusing to poison Polixenes, casting his baby daughter to the crows, and causing his young son to die. And now, the good, sweet queen has died.

When a lord protests the news, Paulina swears to it and then boldly challenges any of them to bring Hermione to life. Paulina berates Leontes. For this death, repentance is useless; only unending despair can be his future.

Leontes urges her to continue. He feels that he deserves every syllable of her bitter, unceasing criticism. A lord chastises Paulina for the bold speech which he deems unsuitable under any circumstances, and Paulina apologizes finally for showing "the rashness of a woman" when she observes Leontes' grief. "What's gone and what's past help/ Should be past grief." Again, she requests punishment but, this time, for *her* error since she caused him to grieve about a matter which he should forget. Paulina asks for the king's forgiveness and promises to stop reminding him about their dead queen, his dead children, or her own lost husband. Clearly, Leontes prefers her truthful speech to her pity. He asks Paulina to lead him to the bodies of his son and wife. After he views them, Leontes wants them to share the same grave, which shall be marked by the shameful causes of their deaths. He promises daily, penitent visits to the chapel where they will be buried.

Commentary

In this scene, Leontes speaks of the contrasts between his reputation for tyranny and Hermione's reputation for noble innocence. Although he claims that he wants the guilt or innocence of Hermione to be proven, obviously the only way that Leontes can be found innocent of the accusations of tyranny would be to prove Hermione is guilty. Determining her guilt or her innocence, however, is a potentially exclusive proposition. Leontes is using a single motivation – jealousy – to prove Hermione guilty in order to prove that he has acted correctly from his sense of "natural goodness." Therefore, Apollo's message will be unacceptable.

The trial itself dramatizes the conflict between "reality" and Leontes' "nature," but this is not a matter of guilt or innocence. This is clearly illustrated in an exchange between Hermione and Leontes. In despair after trying to elicit facts, Hermione says, "My life stands in the level of your dreams." Leontes retorts: "Your actions are my dreams."

Within this structure, the climax of the scene cannot occur with Apollo's message because Leontes must push for his original motivation. Neither facts, as requested by Hermione, nor truth, as delivered from Apollo, will dissuade Leontes.

Leontes is not yet ready for redemption. Although his tyranny has been curbed, he has not earned trust from Hermione and Paulina, who must feel certain that Leontes is now stable enough to be trusted. Hermione has already asked Apollo to control Leontes' sick illusions, and Apollo said that "the king shall live without an heir" (leaving murder of future children a distinct possibility), emphasizing if (not when, if), "that which is lost be not found." This message clearly cannot reassure the ladies.

So, this critical scene sets up the turning point of the plot by requiring the important subplot of rebirth through the healing power of youth. Only then will Order be restored to the Universe.

While the plot is maturing, characterization is also developing. For example, Leontes must suffer for his monumental mistake. He realizes that fact as soon as Mamillius dies: "the heavens themselves/ Do strike at my injustice." Consequently, he realizes that after he destroyed his family and kingdom, he began to destroy the natural Order of the Universe. Realizing that altering the Order will not be treated lightly, the king encourages Paulina to remind him of *why* he suffers throughout his long years of penance.

This realization helps focus on the major motivation for Leontes – that is, he needs to renew his love for his wife and child. Thus, this motivation overrides the one which opened this scene – that is, his vow to prove Hermione guilty. Although the message from Apollo does not change Leontes' jealousy, the news of his son's death shocks him into a realization that he has been wrong and that he has done great harm. This shock climaxes when Paulina announces Hermione's death. Trapped midway between reality and illusion, and shocked by the tragic consequences of his tyranny, Leontes pledges a morbid expression of deep atonement:

> Once a day I'll visit
> The chapel where they lie, and tears shed there
> Shall be my recreation. So long as nature
> Will bear up with this exercise . . .
>
> (III.ii.239-42)

Thus, Leontes must yet learn the full dimension of love and how to express it.

Paulina devotes her life to speaking for the honor of the queen. Interestingly, she seems to recognize the power of subtlety because unlike her previous confrontation with Leontes, here she quickly asks forgiveness for her boldness and rashness with no intention of quitting needling him, as she promises to do.

ACT III – SCENE 3

Summary

Antigonus, who is carrying the hapless royal infant, asks his mariner if they have landed upon "the deserts of Bohemia." The mariner confirms that they have, but he worries about an approaching storm which he interprets as a punishment by the angry heavens. Antigonus orders the mariner to return to take care of the ship and promises to hurry back. The mariner urges Antigonus to stay close to the shore and to hurry and avoid the wild beasts which lurk inland. As Antigonus leaves, the mariner says he will be glad to be finished with this assignment.

Meanwhile, Antigonus talks to the infant about a dream he had the night before. Believing Hermione to be dead, Antigonus describes a nightmarish appearance of the queen's spirit. Like a beautiful "vessel of . . . sorrow," the white-robed spirit approached him, bowed three times, then emitted fury, as a configuration of two spouts projected from her eyes. This dream figure acknowledged that a "fate, against thy better disposition,/ Hath made thy person for the thrower-out/ Of my poor babe." She requested that Antigonus leave the baby in Bohemia and name her Perdita, which means "the lost one." Because of the unpleasant duty that Antigonus had pledged to do, Antigonus will never again see Paulina. Then the spectral figure of Hermione disappeared amidst frightening shrieks.

Antigonus confesses both his fright and his belief that the events seem too real to be called only a dream. Giving full rein to superstition, he interprets that Hermione is dead and that Apollo has directed the baby to the homeland of her real father, Polixenes. But he is not certain of the fate for the baby. So, he blesses her and tenderly lays her down with her few belongings. At that instant, the storm begins.

> Poor wretch,
> That for thy mother's fault art thus exposed
> To loss and what may follow! Weep I cannot,
> But my heart bleeds; and most accursed am I
> To be by oath enjoined to this. Farewell!
> (III.iii.49-53)

Then, seemingly in confirmation of the dream-prophecy, the storm bursts, and a bear chases Antigonus off the stage.

A shepherd enters, grumbling about the useless aggravation caused by boys between the ages of ten and twenty-three. Apparently, he suspects that some youths with the "boiled brains" of this age group have been hunting in the storm and have scared off two of his best sheep.

Suddenly he sees the "very pretty" child, Hermione's daughter. Having already said that boys do nothing but harm, including "getting wenches with child," he assumes this child was born of just such an escapade. Overwhelmed by pity, the shepherd decides to take the baby home. But first, he calls his son, "the clown," to see it: "What, art so near? If thou'lt see a thing to talk on when thou art dead and rotten, come hither." The shepherd notices that his son is upset, so he asks what is wrong.

Two different disasters have shaken the boy. First, during a storm that he describes as encompassing the sea and the sky, he heard the screams and watched the deaths of the entire crew aboard a wrecked ship. Then, someone named Antigonus begged for help as a "bear tore out his shoulder-bone." As the sailors yelled for help, "the sea mocked them," and as Antigonus screamed for help, "the bear mocked him"; eventually, the clown says, all of the victims were "roaring louder than the sea or weather." The shepherd asks when this happened. Just now, responds his son, too soon for the men to be chilled in the sea or the bear to be "half dined on the gentleman."

Both men are distraught at their helplessness. So in contrast, the shepherd draws the clown's attention to "things new-born," and points out "a bearing-cloth for a Squire's child." The shepherd speculates that this baby is a changeling, given to him by fairies to fulfill an old prediction that someday he would be rich.

The clown declares that his father will be rich from the gold which is tucked in the baby's wrapping, but the shepherd warns his son to keep the "fairy gold" a secret; he wants to hasten home without bothering to search any longer for his missing sheep. The clown tells his father to take everything home; he will return to the place where Antigonus was killed. Reasoning that if the bear ate until it was sated, it will no longer be dangerous; the boy wants to see if there is enough left of Antigonus to bury. After commending his son for his goodness, the shepherd asks to be brought to the scene so that he himself can see if enough is left on Antigonus to identify his origins. As they exit, the shepherd says cheerfully, "'Tis a lucky day, boy, and we'll do good deeds on 't."

Commentary

This scene is structured on irony and laced with sardonic humor. Dramatic irony is first evident when Antigonus swears to faithfully carry out the king's order to abandon the baby; the audience, you should remember, knows full well that Leontes has now repented of his tyranny. There is additional irony here because of the old shepherd's vituperative attacks on young men; obviously, *his* son does not conform to the shepherd's notion of the norm. Consider also the many tragedies that preceded the shepherd's finding the baby, contrasted with his simple belief that the fairies dropped both the baby and gold in his pathway in order to make him rich.

From this point until the end of the play, comedy will be threaded throughout the central plot, which focuses primarily on poetic justice. The comedy here is based on Shakespeare's incorporating the astounding and incredible. Consider that in this scene alone, Shakespeare includes noisy thunder, ghosts, an attacking bear, slapstick humor, fairies, and a rags to riches myth!

Another use of the astounding that contributes to the plot involves the fate of Antigonus, of Perdita, and that of the mariners. Antigonus and the crew, of course, must die so that no one can report to Bohemia *who* the infant is, and no one can bring news to Sicilia *where* the infant was abandoned. Since Antigonus did not select Bohemia as his destination prior to embarking from Sicilia, Perdita is now completely abandoned to Fate.

As with all Pastoral Romances, the events in this scene can flourish without insistence upon absolute truth. On the way to the "deserts of Bohemia," Antigonus believes that he experiences a supernatural vision which he incorrectly interprets as proof that Hermione has died and that Perdita was fathered by Polixenes. Equally as confused as Antigonus, the old shepherd irrationally believes that something supernatural guided the fairies to leave him a changeling and the gold for his own fortune.

Another element which is consistent with the genre of Pastoral Romance is Shakespeare's moral lessons about virtue and vice. Both Antigonus and the mariner worry about retribution by the heavens for their participation in the heartless, unwarranted punishment of the infant. And this retribution occurs just after Antigonus leaves the infant, stating "most accursed am I." A hungry bear chases Antigonus off the stage at the very moment that the thunderstorm breaks. This storm would most certainly have been viewed by Elizabethan audiences as a disruption of the Heavenly Order.

Shakespeare's humor softens this horror when the shepherd and clown bury Antigonus because "'Tis a lucky day" which calls for "good deeds." Clearly, these two characters are characterized by their rewards for virtue as surely as Leontes is characterized by his punishment for the absence of such virtue. Significantly, all the fantastic elements are used to save Perdita for the healing role which she must play in order for the major conflict to be resolved.

Realism, here, is achieved through characterization. Antigonus, already established as a kind of man who is reluctant to carry out the king's orders, contributes to the possible survival of the infant by wrapping a substantial amount of gold in her blankets. The gold must have been his own; certainly, it was not provided by the crazed Leontes. Antigonus' foresight *does* attract the attention of the shepherd, and although he believes the superstitious possibility that the baby is a changeling (whom the fairies have used as an instrument to provide riches), the shepherd is also a good man who never considers killing the baby – only keeping the gold. He unwaveringly accepts the responsibility to raise the baby – initially, when he thought it was an abandoned bastard and, later, when he thought that it was an instrument of the fairies.

Probability in the plot depends upon the acceptance of illusion: if Perdita were in the hands of these characters on a seacoast of a place called Bohemia where wild bears roamed at the very moment a vicious storm broke, then this *might* follow. Modern audiences will all surely recognize and forgive this perceived breach of probability.

The scene balances comedy and tragedy nicely, introduces new major characters, and it saves the baby for the resolution of renewal and rebirth. Its final dramatic result is that it places Perdita in the very middle of illusion and reality.

ACT IV – SCENE I

Summary

A Chorus symbolizing Time announces that sixteen years have passed. During those years, Leontes has replaced his jealousy with seclusion, while Florizel (the son of the king of Bohemia) and Perdita have grown up and matured in Bohemia.

Commentary

As in ancient Greek plays, a Chorus substitutes narrative for dramatic action. In addition to preparing the audience for an adult Florizel and Perdita, when next we see them, the narrative transcends the focus from the actions of Leontes to the actions of the Bohemian cast of characters.

ACT IV – SCENE 2

Summary

Polixenes and Camillo enter; they are in the middle of a discussion. The King of Bohemia has asked Camillo to drop his request to return to Sicilia, but Camillo cannot; he urges Polixenes to allow him to return to his beloved Sicilia because the penitent Leontes has requested him to do so. Camillo is growing old; he longs both to die at home and to ease the sorrows of the Sicilian king. Polixenes pleads with Camillo to stay; he claims that the goodness and administrative skills of Camillo can never be equaled. And as for the grief in Sicilia, Polixenes prefers not to be reminded of it.

Edging toward his own problems, Polixenes asks Camillo if he has seen Prince Florizel recently. The king hints that a living son can create as much grief as a dead one. Camillo has neither seen Florizel nor can he guess where the prince goes. He knows only that the prince is often absent and has been neglecting his court duties. The king, however, does know where Florizel goes. Spies have reported that Florizel has been seen dawdling about the home of a shepherd, whose financial circumstances have mysteriously improved. Camillo recognizes the description of this shepherd: his household is said to include a daughter of unusual rarity.

In order to discover why Florizel visits the shepherd's home, suspecting the lure of the shepherd's daughter, Polixenes wants Camillo to accompany him to the site. There, in disguise, they should be able to extract an answer of some kind from the simple shepherd. Camillo agrees to drop his request to return to Sicilia and accompany Polixenes on this mission.

Commentary

This scene begins with the central conflict of the subplot. Its complications include Camillo's presence near the persuasive Polixenes, who opposes Camillo's yearning to return home to Sicilia. Another, later conflict, barely sketched here, will be the conflict between the desire of Polixenes, who wants his son to perform filial and royal duties, and Florizel, who wants only to be with Perdita.

Camillo's characterization remains impressive. He behaves superbly as the able and trusted administrator who always exercises independent judgment. As in the first act, he now struggles with a conflict between his desire to serve both kings who want him and his own stronger personal motivation to return home.

Polixenes is developing into a more manipulative and selfish character than we discerned earlier. However, he cannot be mistaken for an evil villain. Like Leontes, he must confront the question of loyal obedience within a family that he loves, but unlike Leontes, he does not permit a few observations to fester until he becomes mad. Before we leave this scene, note that two favorite Elizabethan dramatic gimmicks are promised for the audience's interest—love and disguise.

ACT IV—SCENE 3

Summary

Autolycus enters singing a bawdy ballad. He interrupts his song to announce that he was once a well-dressed servant to Prince Florizel, but he is now out of service. Now, he collects odds and ends. There are hints that he steals them. With the help of harlots and dice, he has acquired his current attire. His favorite source of income, he says, "is the silly cheat," because he fears punishments for committing truly violent crimes.

His spirits soar as he spots a prize!—who is none other than the kind-hearted clown. The shepherd's son is struggling with calculations on the income from the wool of 1,500 sheep and with his responsibility to buy supplies for the sheep-shearing feast. All the details of this transaction are mixed with thoughts about his family, particularly about his "sister," who is to be the "queen" of the feast. Obviously, they are preparing to entertain a large number of people.

Autolycus goes to work. He grovels on the ground and begs the shocked clown to tear the rags off his back. But the clown protests that Autolycus needs more *on* his back, *not less.* Autolycus insists that the loathsome rags offend him more than his scars from many beatings. He claims that he was beaten and robbed by a footman who forced him to put on these detestable garments.

The gentle, gullible clown assists Autolycus to his feet. However, as Autolycus winces to avoid aggravating his non-existent wounds, he picks the pocket of the clown. When the clown offers him money, Autolycus must, of course, refuse; so, he holds off the clown's charity by insisting that a nearby kinsman will aid him.

Pressed for a description of his robber, Autolycus describes himself. The clown protests against this thief who "haunts wakes, fairs, and bear-baitings."

Declaring himself well enough to walk to his relative's home, Autolycus sends the clown on to complete his errands. As soon as the good man exits, the rogue flaunts the stolen purse, mocks the clown's attempt to buy supplies without money, and declares that he will also cheat the guests at the sheep-shearing festival. Autolycus leaves as he entered, singing.

Commentary

Obviously, this scene mixes comedy and pathos, its humor being tempered by the serious effect of the theft from the kind shepherd's son. It also sets up the causal and time sequences for Perdita's role in the sheep-shearing feast during the spring season. In addition, minor characterization developments occur. Shakespeare adds qualities of gullibility and slow-wittedness to the previously revealed quality of kindness in the clown. But the scene's real intrigue focuses on the clown's confusion of illusion with reality. As Autolycus identifies an illusory rogue by providing his own biography, the clown cries out against this imaginary thief to the real thief, the real Autolycus. And the clown never realizes that he himself is the *real* victim in this scene.

ACT IV – SCENE 4

Summary

Florizel and Perdita enter in the middle of a discussion about their future. Florizel then talks about Perdita's role in the feast. He urges her to abandon her identification as the shepherd's daughter while she has this opportunity to exhibit the mythical and royal qualities that he sees in her. But Perdita rejects the romantic dreams of both her role in the feast and their future as lovers. Although she does not want "to chide at [Florizel's] extremes," she details the sham of their costumes:

> Your high self,
> The gracious mark o' th' land, you have obscured
> With a swain's wearing, and me, poor lowly maid,
> Most goddess-like pranked up.
>
> (IV.iv.7-10)

Indeed, if costumes and pranks were not common to these feasts, she doubts that she could tolerate the sham.

Florizel responds by blessing the time that his falcon flew over her father's land. Perdita, however, expresses her dread at the consequences of their "differences," recognizing that "your greatness/ Hath not been used to fear." Suddenly she trembles from the fear of his father arriving and confronting her for a defense of this liaison.

Defending his point of view with examples from mythology, the prince cites a number of gods who transformed themselves for love. He gallantly argues that no precedent of surprise was "for a piece of beauty rarer,/ Nor in a way so chaste." But Perdita warns Florizel that his determination cannot withstand the power of a king. If King Polixenes opposes their union, either "you must change this purpose,/ Or I my life." Florizel declares that should his father force a choice, Perdita would be his choice. Believing that this assurance will free Perdita from her fears, he urges her to begin her fun at the feast by greeting the approaching guests. Far from feeling assured, Perdita appeals, "O lady Fortune,/ Stand you auspicious!"

Like Florizel, the shepherd urges Perdita to begin acting like the hostess of the feast; but, unlike Florizel, he approaches her with anger and frustration. She compares poorly with his old wife, who prepared all the food, then welcomed and served the guests, in addition to performing a song and dance; whereas, Perdita seems to fail at even serving as a hostess.

Thus, the feast's "queen" begins to greet the strangers; first, she greets King Polixenes and Camillo (in disguise), with an aside to us concerning her father's wish that she serve as hostess. She graciously offers nosegays of rosemary and rue as she welcomes them to the feast. All three exchange meaningful comments about flowers and life as Perdita favorably impresses the disguised king (whom she has so dreaded to meet).

Florizel then hurries Perdita away to dance, praising her until a pretty blush appears on her face. As they observe the lovers, Polixenes and Camillo are charmed by Perdita. The king describes her as beautiful and nobler than her background can explain. Camillo declares her to be "the queen of curds and cream."

The clown, meanwhile, organizes a silly crew into a dance of shepherds and shepherdesses, and Polixenes asks the shepherd about his daughter's dancing partner. The shepherd calls him "Doricles," a worthy young man who obviously loves his daughter; furthermore, he hints at a surprising dowry if the two should marry.

A servant announces that a "pedlar" who sings ballads requests entrance. Declaring himself a song-lover, the clown chortles over the sample verses, and he welcomes the pedlar. Perdita cautions against allowing tunes with "scurrilous words."

The clown admits the rogue Autolycus, who instantly charms all his listeners. The clown promises gifts of lace ribbons and gloves to both of his female companions, and the three of them choose a suitable ballad to sing. Autolycus then leaves with them in order to rehearse the ballad.

More entertainers request permission to perform. The shepherd objects, but Polixenes persuades him to permit them to perform; so they watch a dance of twelve satyrs. This reminds Polixenes that it is time to part the lovers.

He teases his son about missing the opportunity to buy gifts for Perdita. Florizel retorts that Perdita prizes the gifts of love, not trifles. Further baited, the young prince declares his love for Perdita for all to hear. Immediately, the shepherd arranges a betrothal with a dowry "equal to Doricles's wealth."

Polixenes interrupts to inquire if the young man has a father to consult. Florizel snorts that his father does not know of this matter and never shall. Although Polixenes grants that a young man should have a say in the choosing of a wife, he suggests that the joy and consequences should be discussed with a father. The shepherd joins in the entreaty. But Florizel stubbornly refuses.

Angrily, Polixenes rips off his disguise. He severs his son's inheritance, threatens to hang the shepherd, and wants to scar Perdita's bewitching beauty before killing her.

Perdita begs Florizel to return to his duties at court and forget her. The shepherd lashes out at his daughter for ruining him and rushes off. But Florizel arrogantly proclaims all this is but a mild setback. His plans remain unchanged. He *will* marry Perdita.

Camillo intervenes to advise separation until the king's anger subsides. Perdita comments, "How often said, my dignity would last/ But till 'twere known!" Only Florizel remains unmoved by the disasters that he has brought upon everyone, seeing nothing as important as fulfilling his vow to Perdita.

Camillo manages to convince Florizel to leave Bohemia and sail for Sicilia, and thus Camillo can both protect the young people and achieve his own goals. And he also convinces the young prince to marry Perdita, then present this romance to Leontes as part of a representation for a reconciliation mission on behalf of Polixenes.

Perdita joins her common sense to Camillo's arguments that this plan is superior to aimless, poverty-stricken wandering. Beginning to realize that he has to protect his beloved, Florizel seeks more advice from Camillo. First, Camillo says, they must acquire disguises for Perdita and Florizel for the escape from Bohemia.

This opportunity presents itself with Autolycus' entrance. The rogue is bragging about his successful thievery at the festival because of the clown's distracting singing. Only a wailing disruption by the distraught shepherd prevented Autolycus from successfully purse-snatching from the entire group. His celebration of what he managed to get away with, however, is interrupted by the approach of the three escapees. They are discussing effective letters that Camillo can provide. Autolycus fears that they have overheard enough to hang him. But Camillo is interested only in bartering for Autolycus' clothes. As soon as Autolycus recognizes Florizel, he begins scheming again, his schemes fueled by careful observation of the two hasty disguises.

Camillo sends the two young lovers off; then, in an aside, he reveals that he will try to convince Polixenes to follow. Thus, Camillo hopes to see Sicilia again, "for whose sight/ I have a woman's longing."

The delighted Autolycus remains to savor his opportunity to inform the king of the flight. But first, he must decide if this would be an honest deed. After deciding that it would be "more knavery to conceal it," he chooses silence as being more true to his profession.

Then, Autolycus steps aside for another opportunity to make money, for he sees the clown and the shepherd approaching. The clown is arguing that his father should tell the king that Perdita is a changeling, not a legitimate daughter, and show the evidence to the king. The shepherd agrees, but he wants to add an indictment against Florizel's pranks.

Autolycus decides to intervene, but he confuses the simple countrymen with an outburst of nonsense which makes him sound convincingly like a courtier. After saying that the king has sought solace from his grief on board a ship, Autolycus frightens the shepherd and his son into believing that they are slated for horrible deaths. Autolycus then promises to carry their story to the king. The gullible clown convinces his father to pay Autolycus enough to buy his help.

As the two simpletons gratefully wander off toward Florizel's ship, Autolycus lingers on stage and talks to the audience about his plan. He will allow Florizel to consider the evidence and the possible harm that might happen to him. At best, the prince will reward him for the information; at worst, he will free the two men and scorn Autolycus for being too officious.

Commentary

This scene is dominated by the image of renewal. This image dominates all other dramatic elements in preparation for its healing role in resolving the major conflict of the plot. This was the role for which Perdita was saved by heavenly intervention and human heroism in Act III, Scene 3. Now, the remaining act must transport Perdita and her possessions toward Sicilia. This is accomplished by Polixenes' tantrum and by some fast thinking by Autolycus and Camillo.

Florizel's opening speech, dense with the imagery of spring and rebirth, focuses on the hope of renewal which is indigenous to the world of this play.

> These your unusual weeds to each part of you
> Do give a life; no shepherdess, but Flora,
> Peering in April's front. This your sheep-shearing
> Is as a meeting of the petty gods,
> And you the queen on't.
>
> (IV.iv.1-5)

Perdita responds by clinging to reality (as she understands it). Ignorant of her royal heritage and the fact that she is a princess, she counters Florizel's romantic dreams with mundane facts, and she expresses her fears about the consequences of his impulsive obsessions. Without the traditions that justify a costume, she would have "sworn, I think,/ To show myself a glass."

Flower imagery dominates Polixenes' estimation of Perdita. The dominant image of renewal is then extended to a universal idea by his weaving the idea of renewal into humanity and nature, then anchoring it to spring's rebirth. As her first act as "queen" of the feast, Perdita presents rosemary and rue to the guests, symbolizing "grace and re-membrance," flowers which seem fresh for a long time "and savour all the winter long." At this point, Polixenes quizzes Perdita about her prejudice against gillyflowers. Perdita says that she has heard that the multi-colored appearance of these flowers, called by some "Nature's bastards," may be due as much to the skills of the gardener as to the flowers' natural characteristics. Polixenes reminds her that this is part of an art which enhances nature, as in the art of grafting, wherein,

> We marry
> A gentler scion to the wildest stock,
> And make conceive a bark of baser kind
> By bud of nobler race.
>
> (IV.iv.92-95)

But Perdita holds to the purity of nature, tying cycles of nature to cycles of humanity with references to flowers "of middle summer" for "men of middle age" and flowers for virgins with hope as well as for virgins who die without having enjoyed a fulfilling love. She covers the entire cycle of human life with a gentle, wise point of view which impresses her visitors.

Perdita is embarrassed about her long speech, but Florizel adds it to a list that he wants to continue forever—her speech, her singing, and her dancing:

> I wish you
> A wave o' th' sea, that you might ever do
> Nothing but that; move still, still so,
> And own no other function. Each your doing,
> So singular in each particular,
> Crowns what you are doing in the present deeds,
> That all your acts are queens.
>
> (IV.iv.140-46)

Perdita also impresses Polixenes with her unexpected grace and wisdom; in fact, all observers express amazement at her queenly behavior although she insists that they remember that she is only a simple shepherd's daughter. Ironically, Polixenes seems ready to "graft" this delight onto the royal family. But Florizel refuses to inform his father of the betrothal. This proud flaw in his nature serves as an important key to the plot development. Florizel refuses to be moved from his independent stance, and he eventually convinces Perdita that she must marry him. They both agree to serve as ambassadors of peace to Sicilia. These are right choices; therefore, no one is punished for filial impiety or deceit – not Florizel, not Perdita, not Camillo, not Autolycus, not the shepherd, and not even the clown.

By this time, the illusion/reality image is treated as a mirrored irony. No one realizes that Perdita's royal qualities are *real* when Camillo persuades Perdita to play the role of a disguised princess in Sicilia. As for Perdita, who has been trapped between reality and illusion since the end of Act III, the reality of being a "shepherd's daughter," which she believes herself to be, prevents her from accepting a role of royalty. Note that everyone believes that Perdita's natural qualities will provide the needed healing power for a reconciliation between Leontes and Polixenes.

In summary, Camillo has intervened in events in order to achieve one more step in his consistent motivation – that is, to return home to die. Polixenes has manipulated people in order to bend them to his will, and Florizel has maintained a single-minded motivation to marry Perdita. Autolycus, the shepherd, and the clown have acted upon previously established motivations. All have contributed to the eventual success of the trip to Sicilia – the healing renewal.

Perdita contributes the least to the plot development at this point because she is ignorant of her heritage and her potential contribution. But she does remain consistent to her character trait of having an uncommon amount of realistic, common sense.

Although none of these characters are one-dimensional, they are all subordinate of the development of plot. Even Leontes emerges as relatively weak. He did not, like Galileo, cling to truth in spite of opposing opinion; Leontes simply flaunted truth with his incorrect opinion.

Clearly, this long, elaborate subplot enhances the main plot; it is not merely a filler. This scene moves from a recognition of Perdita's unique qualities through the cataclysmic upheaval which removes her from her Bohemian sanctuary to the beginning of her journey back to Sicilia. At this point, the hope of renewal is added to Shakespeare's traditional tragic themes of prosperity and destruction.

ACT V – SCENE 1

Summary

Back in Sicilia, Leontes' subjects are urging him to end his long years of penitence. Cleomenes urges that Leontes "do as the heavens have done, forget your evil;/ With them forgive yourself." But Leontes says that he cannot forgive himself as long as he remembers the virtues of Hermione and feels the absence of an heir. Paulina agrees with him and reminds her king that he killed Hermione.

When Dion suggests that Leontes remarry in order to create another heir, Paulina argues that not only are all women unworthy, but that it's impossible to counter Apollo's oracle. She also counsels Leontes to trust that a worthy heir *will* appear when needed.

In the presence of witnesses, Paulina extracts Leontes' pledge not to remarry until *she* selects the time and person; she envisions an older woman who looks exactly like Hermione at a time "when your first queen's again in breath." Suddenly, they are interrupted by a servant who announces that Prince Florizel has arrived with a beautiful bride. Leontes guesses that the visit has been forced "by need and accident."

Paulina attacks the servant's praise of the princess's beauty because she detects disloyalty to Hermione's superior beauty. The servant, however, apologizes but predicts that all will be similarly affected by this beautiful princess:

> Women will love her, that she is a woman
> More worth than any man; men, that she is
> The rarest of all women.
>
> (V.i.110-12)

During the pause before Florizel's entrance, Paulina reminds her king that Mamillius would have been much like this prince. Leontes lashes: "Prithee, no more; cease. Thou know'st/ He dies to me again when talked of." When Florizel enters, Leontes notes the young man's resemblance to Polixenes, and he praises the beauty of Perdita, but still, he says, he deeply regrets the loss of so many loved ones. The king then repeats his wish to see Polixenes again, and Florizel spins a tale about being here to represent Polixenes, who is too infirm to come himself. He describes Perdita as being the daughter of Smalus of Libya. Claiming that he sent the major portion of his party back to Bohemia after Perdita's weeping departure from Smalus, the young prince then boldly tells a fabricated story about their strange arrival.

As Leontes expresses his envy of Polixenes' wonderful family, a Bohemian lord enters with Polixenes' request that Leontes arrest the disobedient prince and the shepherd's daughter who married him. This lord says that Polixenes is in the city, but has paused to confront the shepherd and the clown.

Florizel protests, "Camillo has betrayed me." The Bohemian lord confirms that Camillo is with Polixenes. Perdita says that she regrets the suffering of her father and the unlikelihood of her marriage being recognized. Leontes regrets that Florizel angered his father and that Perdita failed to qualify for a royal marriage.

Although Florizel has voiced doubts ("The stars, I see, will kiss the valleys first"), he begs Leontes to petition Polixenes for permission to allow him to keep Perdita as his wife. Leontes' eagerness to cooperate, because of his fascination for Perdita, brings a protest from Paulina; "Your eye hath too much youth in 't." The king swears that he thinks only of Hermione when he stares at Perdita.

Commentary

Although chances for "renewal" once seemed impossible, they now seem resolvable. Leontes is almost to be purged of the sickness which once twisted him. Perdita, the lost heir, has returned, although she has not yet been recognized. And Leontes, by sympathizing with the young couple's spirit of love, begins to take steps which can heal most of his past destruction of the spiritual and natural order.

ACT V – SCENE 2

Summary

Autolycus organizes the majority of the events in this scene, which is a great help since it is told in fragments. First, Autolycus questions three gentlemen about proceedings in the nearby palace of Leontes. Gradually, he gathers information about the shepherd's testimony. The first gentleman heard only a vague reference to someone's finding a child; thus, he could not guess from what he saw whether or not Leontes and Camillo gestured in joy or sorrow. A second gentleman knows that people are celebrating because "the king's daughter is found." A third gentleman, steward to Paulina, lists enough evidence to dispel doubt about this truth "pregnant/ By circumstance." All major characters in the royal drama were observed to have behaved with a mixture of joy and sorrow when they learned about all of the sorrows that occurred sixteen years ago and rejoiced at today's news. Now, they are gathering at the site of a remarkably lifelike statue of Hermione to eat dinner, during which they hope to witness new and exciting discoveries.

Autolycus reflects on how close he came to being the one to reveal these facts. When he sees the clown and the shepherd, he observes: "Here come those I have done good to against my will." He acknowledges the clown's favorite reward: "I know you are now, sir, a gentleman born." Autolycus patiently listens to the two men boast that they have been "gentlemen born" for four hours. Then, Autolycus begs them to forgive his transgression and to provide a favorable report to Prince Florizel. Both the clown and shepherd agree because they believe that as "gentlemen" they should be generous. Thus, they invite Autolycus to accompany them in the capacity of a servant to view Hermione's statue.

Commentary

This scene dramatizes the effect of repentance and reconciliation — that is, reward. Leontes has repented and Autolycus has nearly done away with his knavery. All of the major characters are reconciled. Rewards are given to the clown and the shepherd. Their primary reward, the rank of gentlemen, along with the reconciliation accomplished by the recognition of Perdita's royal rank, helps restore order because all are placed in a proper rank for the marriage. Unity with universal order is achieved by unifying most of the straggling elements of the plot.

Narration informs the audience about the reconciliations. All of the emotional scenes occur offstage. But Shakespeare does provide guidelines for action which could be used to enliven the dull narrative: ". . . the king and Camillo/ . . . seemed almost,/ With staring on one another, to tear the cases/ Of their eyes. . . . A notable passion of wonder appeared in them."

ACT V – SCENE 3

Summary

As the celebration party strolls through Paulina's estate on their way to Hermione's statue, Leontes praises the hostess for her years of good service. When Paulina reveals Hermione, who is standing like a statue, the group is stunned into silence. Leontes speaks first of the statue's lifelike appearance, then notes: "Hermione was not so much wrinkled, nothing/ So aged as this seems." Paulina explains that the artist imagined how she would look now. Not surprisingly, Leontes feels rebuked by the lifelike statue. Perdita tries to touch it, but Paulina warns her that the paint on the statue is not yet dry.

Leontes' painful sorrow is so evident that Camillo, Polixenes, and Paulina each try to ease his suffering. Leontes' intense desire for Hermione increases, and when Paulina tries to draw the curtain in front of the statue, she is forbidden to do so by Leontes. Perdita also expresses a desire to continue to look at the statue.

Then Paulina offers to make the statue move if no one accuses her of consorting with evil spirits. Leontes encourages her. Calling for music, Paulina commands Hermione to descend from her pedestal. Leontes touches Hermione and wonders at her warmth: "If this be magic, let it be an art/ Lawful as eating."

Hermione embraces Leontes, and Polixenes and Camillo suddenly wonder aloud if she is alive. When Paulina turns Hermione's attention to Perdita, Hermione speaks. First, she praises the gods, then she asks Perdita how she survived; finally, she states that with hope in the oracle's message, she preserved herself for this very moment.

Paulina blesses the reunited family and then offers to withdraw:

> I, an old turtle [turtledove],
> Will wing me to some withered bough and there
> My mate, that's never to be found again,
> Lament till I am lost.
>
> (V.iii.132-35)

But Leontes forestalls her loneliness by arranging a match with Camillo. After some conciliatory remarks to all aggrieved parties, Leontes organizes a departure to exchange reminiscences.

Commentary

In this scene, Leontes, Camillo, Hermione, and Paulina all *earn* their rewards. In contrast, Polixenes, Florizel, and Perdita *receive* their rewards.

The thematic confusion of illusion with reality is best illustrated by the statue. This time, Leontes errs by confusing the real Hermione with her illusory role as a lifeless statue: "The fixture of her eye has motion in 't,/ As we are mocked with art." Magic is mentioned, but the reality is its own miracle.

Because of the general repentance, reconciliation and rewards and the specific reunion of family and friends, the ending is more clearly an element of the Romance than being in the genre of Comedy, History, or Tragedy. In the conclusion, the concept of renewal is added to the themes of prosperity and destruction which are more typical of Shakespearean tragedies. Thus, after Leontes has passed through sufficient years of repentance, he and all other major parties are poised for reconciliation, rewards and, above all, the renewal of their families. This renewal (the reuniting of a family) is precipitated by the daughter – a feature this play has in common with the other "problem plays." Symbolic of this renewal is the resurrection of Hermione.

Reminiscent of the sadness, as well as the joy that love brings in the "problem plays" is Paulina's dirge to her brave, dead husband, Antigonus. Although love and marriage dominate the action, this reminder of all the suffering endured by the loving family and friends since the beginning of the play haunts the observer. Yet, perhaps the entire possibility of a happy ending is suspect. Even when reality seems in focus again, Shakespeare confronts us with the unprovable illusion/reality controversies of resurrection and rebirth. Allusion to seasonal cycles of rebirth as a part of nature cannot prove within the world of this play that all destruction is a part of a cycle of rebirth. Time is still a shadow, and the play ends with memories of the world's mixture of illusion and reality, happiness and sadness, love and hate. Any of these lovers is capable of inflicting destruction and grief on their loved ones.

But from the thematic perspective, with all characters now correctly exercising the use of Free Will, they are expected to contribute to (and benefit from) the orderly maintenance of the universe. Their exit is an orderly representation of the Cosmic Dance and level of the Heavenly Order coming together in harmony.

REVIEW QUESTIONS

1. Romantic conventions appear in many sections of *The Winter's Tale*. Name three influences on events at the sheep-shearing feast. Identify Romantic conventions in relation to some settings in this play. Comment on any which might have damaged the ending of this play.

2. Is Leontes the same loving husband and friend at the end of this play as he was at the beginning? If not, why not?

3. How does Shakespeare use characterization to threaten, then save, the infant Perdita? Use quotations if they help.

4. Describe how Shakespeare sets up and resolves the basic problem in this play.

5. Identify at least three parallels between the main plot and the subplot in *The Winter's Tale*. Is the effect an enhancement or a redundancy?

6. How does Autolycus gather passengers into the boat which is sailing from Bohemia?

7. Identify the major conflict in *The Winter's Tale*. How is the conflict resolved?

8. How probable are the events in Act V?

9. Paulina has often been described as a character whose actions grow from motivation. What is her motivation? Is she likable?

10. Is it unrealistic to portray a man, like Leontes, who kills indiscriminately because of unjustifiable jealousy?

SELECTED BIBLIOGRAPHY

ADAMS, J. Q. *A Life of William Shakespeare*. Boston: Houghton Mifflin Co., 1923.

ALLEN, RALPH G. and JOHN GASSNER, eds. *Theatre and Drama.* 2 vols. Boston, 1964.

ARMSTRONG, EDWARD A. *Shakespeare's Imagination.* Lincoln: University of Nebraska Press, 1963.

BENTLEY, GERALD E. *Shakespeare: A Bibliographical Handbook.* New Haven: Yale University Press, 1961.

BRADBROOK, M. D. *Elizabethan Stage Conditions.* Cambridge: The University Press, 1968.

CHAMBERS, E. K. *William Shakespeare.* New York: Oxford University Press, 1930.

CLEMEN, WOLFGANG. *The Development of Shakespeare's Imagery.* New York: Hill and Wang, 1951.

CREIZENACH, WILHELM. *The English Drama in the Age of Shakespeare.* Reprint of 1916 edition. Boston: Dynamic Learn. Corp., 1979.

ELLIS-FERMOR, UNA. *Shakespeare the Dramatist and Other Papers,* ed. Kenneth Muir. New York: Barnes & Noble, Inc., 1961.

FALCONER, A. F. *Shakespeare & The Sea.* Bungay, Suffolk: Richard Clay and Company, Ltd., 1964.

FREY, CHARLES. *Shakespeare's Vast Romance: A Study of The Winter's Tale.* Columbia: University of Missouri Press, 1980.

FURNESS, HORACE HOWARD, ed. *The Winter's Tale: A New Variorum Edition of Shakespeare.* New York: Dover Publications, Inc., 1964.

JOSEPH, BERTRAM. *Acting Shakespeare.* New York: Theatre Arts, 1969.

JOSEPH, SISTER MIRIAM. *Rhetoric in Shakespeare's Time: Literary Theory of Renaissance Europe.* New York: Harcourt, Brace & World, Inc., 1962.

KOKERITZ, HELGE. *Shakespeare's Names: A Pronouncing Dictionary.* New Haven: Yale University Press, 1959.

MCFARLAND, THOMAS. *Shakespeare's Pastoral Comedy.* Chapel Hill: The University of North Carolina Press, 1972.

PARROTT, THOMAS MARC and ROBERT HAMILTON BALL. *A Short View of Elizabethan Drama.* New York: Charles Scribner's Sons, 1958.

RIGHTER, ANNE. *Shakespeare and the Idea of the Play.* Harmondsworth, Middlesex: Penguin Shakespeare Library, 1967.

SPURGEON, CAROLINE. *Shakespeare's Imagery.* London: Cambridge University Press, 1965.

TILLYARD, E. M. W. *The Elizabethan World Picture.* New York: Vintage Books.

WILLIAMS, JOHN ANTHONY. *The Natural Work of Art: The Experience of Romance in Shakespeare's Winter's Tale.* Cambridge, Massachusetts: Harvard University Press, 1967.

WILSON, JOHN DOVER. *Life in Shakespeare's England,* "Rogues and Vagabonds," pp. 296-317. Harmondsworth, Middlesex: Penguin Books, 1951.

NOTES

NOTES

NOTES

NOTES

NOTES

NOTES